For Elisabeth and Norman
with all the love and affection
from Aldo Maria and Carlo
16 Dec 1995

Living in

PORTUGAL

Anne de Stoop
Preface by Mário Soares
Photography by Jérôme Darblay
Assisted by Caroline Champenois

Flammarion
Paris - New York

Translated by Francis Cowper
Copyediting by
Christine Schultz-Touge
Proof reading by Bernard Wooding
Visitor's Guide translated by
Glenn Naumovitz

Editorial direction: Ghislaine Bavoillot
Designed by Marc Walter
Origination by Colourscan, France
Typesetting by Octavo Editions, Paris
Printed in Italy by Canale, Turin

Flammarion
26, rue Racine
75006 Paris

ISBN: 2-08013-567-8
Numéro d'édition: 0932
Dépôt légal: March 1995

For Martine and Antonio
Anne de Stoop

In memory of Água de Peixes
Jérôme Darblay

CONTENTS

PREFACE

by Mário Soares

It is perhaps impossible to define the Portuguese art of living, a nuanced art that is beyond words, as this "Angel of Silence" seems to suggest. The elegance and delicacy of this symbol belong to the Portuguese people as a whole. Probably painted at the end of the eighteenth century, it is to be found in the chapel of the Santos Palace, also known as the Abrantes Palace, which houses the French embassy in Lisbon.

This book is one in a collection intended to introduce the reader to the customs, traditions, cultural and natural riches, and lifestyles of various countries. As such it is a fine traveler's guide to Portugal, providing an excellent itinerary for anyone wanting to get to know the country better.

From Portugal's natural heritage and landscapes to its architecture and history; from gastronomy to the popular arts; from music to painting and, above all, literature—even though not exhaustive—this book indicates for each region and each town all of the most significant aspects and things most worth seeing.

While it has many of the characteristics of a tourist guide, the book actually goes further. Its careful cultural references, with quotations from writers and artists, and the information it contains make it a brief but useful introduction for all who would like to know about Portugal or are planning a visit.

Portugal is a country with a long history and a rich and original culture open to many influences. Notwithstanding its great diversity of people and landscapes, it succeeds in maintaining a remarkable degree of national identity.

It is a European country, but it stands both on the shores of the Atlantic, which softens its climate, and at the mouth of the Mediterranean, which marks its character. In the fifteenth century Portugal launched into the maritime adventures of the Age of Discoveries, giving Europe a gateway onto the world. Layered as it is with diverse influences, and having integrated a variety of cultures and customs, Portugal—one of the oldest states in Europe, with borders that have remained unaltered since the thirteenth century—has managed to preserve its own very particular identity over the ages. It was the first European country to build a vast empire—which went from Malaysia and India to the coasts of Africa and Latin America, taking in Brazil as well as a number of Atlantic islands—and the last to abandon it. This adventure, which has spanned six centuries, has given us a common language spoken by almost two hundred million people, and an original intermixing of cultures marked by a great sense of universalist humanism and fraternity, regardless of race or religion.

Today Portugal is a country open to modernity, democracy, and a respect for human rights. It emerged from a long dictatorship with the peaceful and bloodless "Carnation Revolution" of 25 April 1974. Portugal joined the European Community in 1985, resuming an old tradition of democracy that dates from the very origins of the nation in 1140. It has embraced the values of peace and solidarity, in the belief that a better understanding between peoples and an exchange of cultures are irreplaceable factors for human enrichment and mutual respect with a tolerance for that which is different.

The collection to which this book belongs is conceived in a similar spirit of openness, to develop better understandings of things that are foreign to us. For this reason I am pleased to write these words of introduction, and to convey my best wishes to author and publisher alike.

Mário Soares

Presidencia da Republica,
Palacio de Belém, Lisbon, July 1994

A COUNTRY WITH A GENTLE WAY OF LIFE

"**A**ll that must be white is pure white," remarked Jean Giraudoux in his book entitled *Portugal*. In the immense Alentejo plain, villages rise up like mirages. The dazzling white of the walls contrasts with the gray schist of paving slabs which, in their rough simplicity, recall all of the violence of the local terrain. Here whitewashed houses look like sculptures made of earth, lime, and light (left, at Monsaraz).

To attempt to present Portugal in just a few lines is surely a rash undertaking. How can judgment be passed on a country that you love, a country that so excels in making life an art? Should its mystery be left intact, or all of its wonders shouted from the housetops?

Simply the sound of spoken Portuguese fills you with a desire to be there. The slightly melancholic accent, the surprising intonations, the mystery of the phonetics, and the abundant richness and musicality of this language of poets are a delightful invitation to travel.

You very quickly discover that this country is profoundly different from its neighbor. "Spain and Portugal live on the same peninsula, but back to back rather than face to face," Michel Déon stressed. Portugal has, for a very long time, been a world unto itself. Established as a nation almost eight hundred years ago, it is the oldest European country still within its original borders. It was also the first nation of Europe to have a single unified language. This long history is one of the keys to understanding a country that became conscious of its unique character very early on.

With its back to Spain, and its long front bordered by the Atlantic, Portugal has always faced outward. "It is easy to understand how, from the heart of the huge Alentejan plain, there emerged a faith and hope in a national destiny which had the world as its stage," noted the writer Miguel Torga. "It was necessary to part from these successive waves of earth without shipwrecks and without chasms in order to be able to go confidently towards the sea."

All of Portugal's history thus becomes a homage to the Age of Discoveries, an adventure beginning in the fifteenth century that so profoundly shaped the country. Portuguese sailors were forever heading off into the unknown—first timidly down as far as Morocco, then moving from inlet to inlet round to the Cape of Good Hope, and finally all the way to Japan and Brazil.

According to Fernando Pessoa, all Portuguese carry within them a certain nostalgia for the grandeur of the past. This bittersweet melancholy, a part of everyday life, is known as *saudade*—"a pain that you enjoy, a pleasure from which you suffer," in the words of the poet Francisco Manuel de Mello. It can also be defined as a longing for a happiness that is never satisfied, mingled with a certain nostalgia for the future.

Getting to know Portugal means going from one surprise to another. In winter a white mantle covers the ground: a coating of snow on the Serra da Estrêla, a carpet of almond blossoms in the Algarve—this country loves contrasts. In the north, a verdant land drenched with rain, the sun pierces light mists that come in from the ocean. The atmosphere is often bathed in a poetic pearl-gray light. Here the Atlantic ocean is never far away.

"I have sometimes thought that Portugal could be called Atlantis," remarked the writer A. T'Serstevens. "Its climate, its vegetation, its coastal life and even its agriculture, its history, discoveries, and conquests, its very own Manueline architecture, a large part of its literature, race, character, and language can be summed up in one single word: Atlantic."

However, in the province of Alentejo—*Além Tejo* "beyond the Tagus"—the cool, temperate climate of the seacoast seems a long way away. Here harsh cold winters follow the burning heat of summer. This is no longer the Atlantic, but already the Orient. To see this you need only travel to the Algarve, a region permanently bathed in sunshine, where the blue sky, the clear air, and a fabulous light make it an immensely attractive region.

The houses, with their brilliant white walls, seem to spring from the atmosphere that surrounds them. In this part of the country everything is colorful, even the sun-drenched white of façades. The corners of houses, plinths, cornices, and window frames are often edged with ochre, bordered in blue, painted in green, or highlighted in red. By the use of contrasting effects, color accentuates or corrects the shapes of buildings, becoming an integral part of the structure itself. Color adorns entire walls in seaside towns, particularly yellow ochres, but also pinks, reds, and pale greens. It can even be found on the granite houses of the north, made iridescent by verdant lichen, turned golden by the sun, washed out by the rain, or set off by traditional two-toned window frames.

However, the most characteristic aspect of the use of color in Portugal are azulejos, the amazing faïence tiles. With its azulejos this land of poets has taught the world to make dreams of their everyday life. For more than five hundred years, under the combined influence of the Moors and that of their Spanish neighbors, the Portuguese have been reinventing this décor, which now transforms the interiors of religious buildings and of houses, decorates gardens and patios, and takes over façades. For Paul Morand, "these azulejos find a place for themselves everywhere—in the private chapels of palaces . . . in aristocratic antechambers, as a faint pink extension of salon lamps; or in gardens on the backs of benches, and under the waters of basins . . . They give life to the austerity of trimmed hedges, make the green of lawns sing out, spread their rare colors with a boldness that sometimes borders on licentiousness." And they always succeed in captivating, in casting a spell, whether they are telling a story in the Western narrative tradition or whether they are composing artful geometric patterns, a song that is almost an incantation in the image of the Orient.

The Occident ceaselessly turned towards the Orient—this is definitely one of Portugal's greatest appeals. Ancient Rome already had a presence here, at the remarkable site of Conimbriga. Later, in the Middle Ages, there was a flowering of Romanesque and Gothic abbeys, which were the pride of Christianity. Then, over the centuries, the architecture evolved, enriched by elements deriving from the Italian Renaissance, from baroque, rococo, and a nationalist eclecticism. Prestigious monuments can be discovered everywhere. The churches and monasteries of Alcobaça, Batalha, Tomar, Évora, of São Roque and Graça in Lisbon, the palaces of Vila Viçosa, Queluz and Mafra, and the Bom Jesus staircase near Braga.

The Portuguese temperament is fundamentally baroque, just as the French spirit is notably classical. Lusitanian architecture has a specificity shared with the Portuguese language: a freedom of form and a profusion of ornament favoring sensibility and imagination. This constant tendency towards baroque expression came to full fruition at the end of the fifteenth century with Manueline art, conceived within the aura of wealth and glory that prevailed under the reign of Dom Manuel. At the monastery of the Hieronymites at Belém, and at those of Batalha and Tomar, the imagination of the artists as applied to late-Gothic structures seems to be heightened by the discoveries that were being made across the world at that time.

Also typically baroque was the profusion of *talha dourada* in the eighteenth century. This carved wood, gilded with the gold that was flooding in from Brazil, invaded retables and sometimes even whole churches with an incredible ardor—notably the church of São Francisco in Oporto. Soon, particularly in the north of the country, the façades

The resplendent costumes of Minho are among the most beautiful in Portugal. Brightly colored vests, skirts, and embroidered wool aprons are worn with blouses and white stockings. They can be seen in the succession of religious festivals and pilgrimages that take place from spring through late autumn, of which the best known is that of Our Lady of the Agony at Viana do Castelo. Processions follow one after the other with a festive Minhoto freedom. The shooting of fireworks and rockets called *foguetes* is accompanied by folk dancing (right, a festival near Ponte de Lima).

According to Paul Morand: "Portugal is the kingdom of glazed clay, faïence having been for its former Arab masters what porcelain was to Cathay. Whereas in Andalusia azulejos are sober, in Portugal they are bold with brash mauves, strident yellows, scenes from legends, portraits, sea battles, poems, and landscapes. Thanks to azulejos Lusitanian history can be read in the open air." These characteristic faïence tiles are part of the Portuguese landscape. Particular care is taken with the borders of tiled panels (left, the Casa Anadia, near Mangualde).

also began to take on curves, and stonework was transformed into vigorous vegetal forms driven by a rococo dynamic. In the nineteenth century the "revivalist" style gave new life to this dynamic. This tendency towards the baroque—the *barocco,* a word created by the Portuguese, meaning "irregular pearl"—finds particular expression in the art of landscape gardening. In the south, where the climate is milder, walled gardens act as an extension of houses, and hide behind high walls. Through their artifice the azulejos of gardens often outdo Nature and colorfully dress up decorative arches and benches. The gardens of the north are more open to nature, less secret and more monumental, with granite statues, large fountains, and vegetal sculptures in the form of arcades, bowers, benches, birds, and serpents created from camellias and box.

These gardens are always in the image of some original Eden, a paradise that this profoundly religious people continually dreams of. As evidence of this you have only to travel the country's roads and watch pilgrims making their way to Fatima, the sanctuary that for many represents the mystical heart of Portugal. Here the sense of the spiritual is expressed by a religion that has managed to stay close to the people and each gesture is laden with symbolism. Here we find the *romaria* pilgrimages, processions, and *alminhas*—small folk shrines located by the sides of roads. And then there are also rosaries seen hanging in taxis, and the name *Maria,* in homage to the Virgin, which is found everywhere—on ceramics, boats, trucks, bread loaves, and even rice puddings, where it is delicately traced with cinnamon powder.

This faith is a crucial element in understanding the temperament of the Portuguese, built on immediate fraternity and openness. Here you feel that it is never a problem to be different. Could this be the secret of the Portuguese art of living?

When you put this kind of question to the Portuguese, they are amused. They tell you that this art is impossible to define, given that the Portuguese temperament is such a complex thing. The way of living in a country with such a long-standing history and culture could perhaps best be defined as a way of living in society. The Portuguese are exquisitely polite, and many countless nuances are to be found in the *tratamento.* There are multiple ways of addressing other people in everyday speech, but it is most often and quite naturally done in the third person—a royal pleasure that makes a change from the tedious dictatorship of excessive familiarity.

In Portugal making guests feel welcome is a national tradition. Here hospitality is always marked by infinite charm. In fact this nation, driven by necessity towards foreign lands, has always had an astonishing ability to adapt. This fascination with other countries, and the ability to learn languages, make it an extraordinarily hospitable country. Already in the sixteenth century the traveler-poet Camões sang the praises of the immensity of a Portugal enlarged by dialogue with other civilizations, making his country the founding terrain of today's universalism.

An enjoyment of social life explains the Portuguese fondness for coming together at meals. Gastronomic pleasures are enhanced by this everyday ritual of sharing life's ups and downs with family or friends. Portugal's farmers and sailors are experts at supplying the best produce of land and sea, and certain dishes even mix meat with shellfish, in a highly symbolic synthesis.

Life in Portugal has many facets. The aim of this book is to present the pleasures and delights of everyday life, rather than a resumé of the country's history and its principal monuments. Let us discover these charms by traveling the country from north to south—leaving out Madeira and the Azores, which are a world unto themselves. Our journey invites us to contemplate landscapes shaped by light and color, to stroll in extraordinarily diverse towns and villages, to dream in gardens, to savor delicious foods and wines, to discover local arts and crafts, while being privileged guests in palaces, *quintas,* manor houses, and *montes* that illustrate this special lifestyle so well.

Minho and Douro

The Wine-producing Regions

A delicately illuminated angel watches over the chapel of the manor house of Calheiros. Such wonderful *talhas* of carved wood, usually painted or gilded, strive to transform every altar into a reflection of the kingdom of God (preceding double page).

How green is the province of Minho, the cradle of Portugal (far right). Tall stacks of straw dotting the countryside indicate a pastoral civilization (top). Granite pillars support arbors so high that ladders must be used for the harvest. The pillars sometimes support clotheslines for drying the laundry (middle).

This is cattle-raising territory, and oxen are every farmer's pride. Their carved yokes are veritable works of art (bottom).

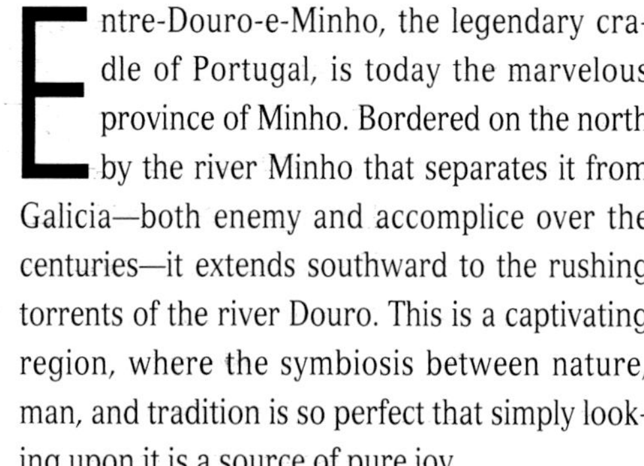

Entre-Douro-e-Minho, the legendary cradle of Portugal, is today the marvelous province of Minho. Bordered on the north by the river Minho that separates it from Galicia—both enemy and accomplice over the centuries—it extends southward to the rushing torrents of the river Douro. This is a captivating region, where the symbiosis between nature, man, and tradition is so perfect that simply looking upon it is a source of pure joy.

"Here the green tints outdo the colors of the rainbow," wrote Miguel Torga, the patriarch of Portuguese literature. The Minhoto countryside presents a complex mosaic of greens, a poetic marquetry which is enhanced by the diffuse luminosity and the fact that the air is charged with humidity from the ocean. Over the centuries this mountainous region, so much a symbol of the energy of the local people, has become a garden in which every inch of land has been cultivated. The wide valleys, with their fields and terraced pastures, climb gently to the heights. The sound of murmuring water is everywhere. Whether wild or domesticated, it feeds wash houses and fountains, irrigates cornfields, gurgles along in little gullies, and sometimes funnels down through curious channels, built up in the middle with stones, that serve as both streams and paths.

There is more green—a luminescent emerald—to be found in the *vinhas de enforcado,* which are hanging, climbing vines grown at the edge of fields, sometimes assuming giant proportions, stringing from tree to tree, twining round fences and posts, and creating a curtain of green along roadsides. Often they create veritable cathedrals of foliage. These *latadas*—immense trellises extending horizontally and supported on impressive monolithic granite posts—supply shade for the plants that grow under them, such as potatoes, kidney beans, broad beans, or the amazing velvety-green cabbages that are Portugal's national vegetable. These hardy vines produce the lively, slightly sugary, slightly acid sparkling wine known as *vinho verde.* In autumn, when the countryside is alive with the sound of laughter and song, the grape pickers bring tall, lightweight eucalyptus-wood ladders, which they lean against trees to reach the vines.

The grapes are picked before they are fully ripe to produce *vinho verde,* a wine with a low alcohol content—as opposed to that made from mature grapes called *maduro.* This, and not its color, accounts for its being called *verde.* In fact the most common *vinho verde* is *tinto,* a red wine with a flavor of unripe fruit and a surprising metallic taste. This unusual rustic beverage is popular in the countryside, where it is drawn from the barrel and served in bowls at small village taverns. While the red *tinto* continues to be produced in traditional vineyards, the white *vinho verde* has proved so successful that it is being cultivated increasingly on trained vines. Deprived of its freedom in these soberly policed vineyards, the wine loses something of its fresh acidity.

Wine is, in a sense, the heart and soul of the Minho, this smiling region of rich harvests. Occasionally it is still possible to hear the ancient creaking of carts with solid wooden wheels, drawn by pairs of oxen whose huge, lyre-shaped horns seem to stretch towards the sky. On certain days, when such a bucolic transport suddenly appears around the bend or through the sunlit branches of a vine-bordered road, the Minho easily compares to the gardens of Arcadia.

However, this garden has a frontier: the Serra do Marão mountain range that separates it from another world, the province of Trás-os-Montes—literally "beyond the mountains"—where the Upper Douro flows. This hot valley region, situated far into the hinterland, was the birthplace of port wine, now famous throughout the world. It offers one of the finest landscapes transformed by human hands to be found anywhere.

Confined in a deep valley, the Douro flows down between steeply sloping mountains. These

escarpments, where the terraces, or *socalcos,* are kept in place by high, dry stone walls called *calços,* have all the majesty of ancient Assyrian ziggurats. The horizontals of the *socalcos* and the verticals of the *calços,* which can be up to five meters high, shape the landscape like rippling furrows. Depending on the season, these sculpted mountains glow in various shades of green, gold, purple, brown, and beige. They also change color according to the light—brightened by the rising sun, contoured at midday, carved by low evening rays, shaped in the moonlight, veiled by mist, or softened in the fog.

The human efforts required to tame this obstinate realm of nature seem to rival those of God. But why put so much work into it? Miguel Torga spoke eloquently of the terrible paradox of this rugged, poor soil, with its difficult climate and its mountainous terrain, producing a wine that is so sweet, the wine that is known as *vinho generoso:* "No stream in our country flows in a harder bed, or finds such determined obstacles, or has to struggle so much along its route; no other corner of our country has such vast fallow lands, at once fertile and damned. . . . In summer a furnace-like heat scorches the schist and transforms the stream into a nightmare of molten lava; in winter, even the eye-shoots of plants cry with the cold. . . . But this was what Titan taught humanity: to be new creators of life on this arid, hostile soil; to give a daily reply to death; to transform each hillside into a parapet of hope, and each drop of sweat into a drop of sweet wine."

But here too, as in the Minho, the countryside is gradually changing. The traditional low walls are giving way to terraces held in place by diagonal embankments. And a new method of planting perpendicular to contour lines is being tried so that harvesting can be mechanized. Is this a risky gamble, or simply the solution of the future?

Further inland, where the terrain is still as mountainous as ever, the province of Trás-os-Montes reveals itself in all the purity once described so passionately by Miguel Torga: "I shall tell you of a wonderful kingdom. . . . What you will need to see it are eyes that have not lost their original innocence in the face of reality, and a heart that does not hesitate . . . first you see an ocean of stones. Wave after wave of them, staggered, upstanding, and hostile." But sometimes villages also appear, so densely packed, with their stone walls and thatched roofs, that they seem to have sprung directly from the soil of this austere and arid terrain.

Having traveled through miles, is it possible that you have also traveled through time? In this imposing region, with its rugged climate, everything is dignified, noble, and pure. Even the air has an extraordinary transparency. Further to the north, the Gerês mountain range in Minho province is covered with splendid sites and forests rich in wildlife. Eagles and wild horses abound here in the Peneda-Gerês national park, one of the finest eco-museums in Europe.

TOWNS AND VILLAGES OF SCHIST AND GRANITE

What a wonderful experience it is to travel through northern Portugal. The mountains, hills, wide valleys, and broad estuaries change almost

"More than a third of Portugal is covered by forests which, with remarkable patience and tenacity, have been restored after the devastation of previous centuries, when the requirements of Portugal's sailing ships devoured the timber stocks of entire regions," wrote Michel Déon. Suffused with light, the *serra* of Alvão, with its forests of tall, hundred-year-old trees, bears witness to this fact (far left).

In this country where ceramics are king, charming terra-cotta finials can be found, such as this dove that seems to be cooing on the edge of a roof (top).

Water bubbles up out of the granite everywhere. It flows in narrow rivulets and

threads its way to local homes, but it is also capable of carving deep valleys, like those of the Vez, the Tâmega, and the Lima, where one can fish for trout and lamprey (middle and bottom).

day by day with the never-ending round of the seasons, and offer the visitor a plethora of towns, bustling villages, and poetic hamlets. Stone, whether whitewashed or left bare, makes its presence felt everywhere. As Fernand Pouillon wrote in *Les Pierres sauvages:* "The light seems to lay down by turns the colors of the spectrum, shades of gray, flooded with sunlight. The crude stone blocks plucked from the earth become noble matter; each strike, each visible fragment, bears witness to energy and perseverance."

The coastline has a number of busy ports which owe their existence to the Age of Discoveries. Over the years, Viana do Castelo became covered by granite houses with monumental emblazoned doorways, then by the houses of the "Brazilians"—the Portuguese who made their fortunes in Brazil during the nineteenth century. Here, in this capital of the deep-sea fishing industry, one can sit in a charming arcaded square and taste the local cod specialty, the *bacalhau à Margarida da Praça.* River fish are equally valued in these estuary ports. This is the land of shad and succulent lampreys from the river Minho, which are accompanied by a cool, slightly sparkling *vinho verde.*

The valley of the river Lima, which has the serenity of one of Poussin's classical landscapes, is lined with pleasant market towns. Ponte de Lima, Ponte da Barca and, further along, Arcos de Valdevez, are located on traditional through routes, as their names suggest. Ponte de Lima is best discovered by strolling down its narrow streets. Here, bare or whitewashed granite reigns and the stone is carefully worked into Gothic arches, Manueline rope motifs, mannerist pediments, and baroque window frames. A Portuguese writer, the count of Aurora, sang the praises of Monday mornings when the town is transformed: "Oh, stranger, if you could only come on a market day. . . ." Early in the morning, in a halo of sun and dust, the sight of entire flocks of sheep crossing the narrow bridge over the

A gentle breeze blows across the banks of the Lima, where bed linen is hung out to dry (left). The north is known for its unbleached linen, once woven at home. Today linen, like cotton, is produced in the factories that are scattered throughout the countryside.

The staircases, doorways, and window frames of the Minho province give full expression to the beauty of granite (top). This superb pediment decorates the chapel of the manor of Calheiros (bottom).

Lima presents an image that is positively biblical. At the river's edge, a poetic sea of rectangular white umbrellas provides shelter for the stallholders and merchants who come in to town from the surrounding area.

Lunch can be enjoyed in a small local restaurant; particularly recommended is a rustic specialty that originated in Ponte de Lima, the *arroz de sarrabulho.* This rice dish, which is prepared with pork and pig's blood, has become a regular offering in the gastronomic traditions of the region. The *rojões à moda do Minho* also provide a delightful summary of the region's products: pork, potatoes, chestnuts, blood, and giblets. These dishes are usually eaten with a delicious golden-colored corn bread, the *broa de milho,* together with a glass of the red *vinho verde tinto* of Ponte de Lima, which is appreciated for its fruity, fresh, slightly tannic taste. For dessert there is the *aletria com ovos,* a local delicacy made with egg yolk and sugar. During Easter the pastry shops produce cakes called *folares da Páscoa,* in the shape of birds' nests with eggs covered by a pastry cross, symbolizing the Resurrection.

These characteristic products of the region are found in all the markets, but one of the best-stocked is that of Barcelos, held on Thursdays. Everybody knows this market, even as far afield as Lisbon. Here you can find all the produce of the region. As in every market, this is where peasants come to bring their livestock—the wealth and pride of the Minhotos. Farmers come to sell cackling poultry, as well as vegetables and fruit that are stacked in fragrant, multicolored pyramids. Agricultural and modern domestic implements of every kind sit side by side with traditional artifacts such as besom brooms.

Since Barcelos is one of the major centers of artisanal production in Portugal, it is an ideal place to go shopping. The fine bobbin laces, towels, the *colchas* (hand-woven linen bedspreads) and the multicolored flower-embroidered tablecloths of Viana do Castelo exemplify a textile tradition that is still very much alive in the north. Wooden ox yokes, masterpieces of popular art, either carved or with openwork and sometimes painted in bright colors, sit next to simple rustic toys, copperware, and baskets. Apart from the ever-present symbol of the cockerel, there are various eye-catching ceramics in glazed terra cotta including figurines, as well as the strange religious and profane characters produced by the ceramist Julia Ramalhão. Although extremely rustic, the glazed crockery produced with this modest red clay and painted with yellow motifs often strikes the eye as extraordinary.

Such a hymn to Portugal could rightly be sung in Guimarães. It was here that Alfonso Henriques declared the country's independence from Castile in 1139, which marked the founding of the free kingdom of Portugal. This thriving town has somehow managed to preserve the architectural heritage of its squares, with their medieval houses and eighteenth-century residences. These substantial buildings with garreted roofs feature wide windows fronted with wrought-iron grilles. One of the most astonishing monuments is the palace of the dukes of Bragança, which was almost entirely rebuilt in the Salazarist style of the 1930s.

The most beautiful town in the region is undoubtedly Braga, the two-thousand-year-old capital of the Minho province. In this ancient religious city, palaces sit side by side with opulent churches, wide squares, fountains, and gardens full of camellias. Devotees of rococo art will discover jewels such as the Casa do Raio, which was inspired by the rococo palaces of Germany.

On the banks of the river Tâmega, Amarante, with its wooden-balconied houses, is another town that keeps traditions alive, especially those of its pastry shops. The practice of offering *bolos de São Gonçalo,* on the occasion of the *romaria* of the town's patron saint, derives from an ancient custom that was thought to improve one's marriage prospects.

Sitting on the banks of the river Tâmega (top), Amarante's Wednesday market is always animated. Its pastries, made with eggs and sugar, are famous. These include *foguetes* and *bolos de São Gonçalo,* which, by ancient custom, young men and women give to each other on the feast day of Saint Gonçalo.

In the Amarante market one can also find the delicious *biscoitos da Teixeira,* which are square cakes made with honey and cinnamon (middle).

The glazed terra-cotta pottery found in local markets is used for the preparation of regional recipes. To make them heat-resistant, the dishes are rubbed with garlic and filled with boiling water and vinegar before their first use. Especially suitable for cooking rice dishes such as *arroz de forno* (baked rice)—they also make a lovely presentation (bottom).

In Portugal, markets provide the rhythm of everyday life. That of Barcelos is one of the oldest in the country. Beneath tall trees, a forest of white tents shelters the stallholders who gather there on Thursdays throughout the year (far left).

Trás-os-Montes, a province where harsh mountainous terrain alternates with plunging ravines, was home to the region's celebrated writer the late Miguel Torga, who sometimes found an "oasis of peace in the restlessness that has carved out so many geological wrinkles; an immense valley, of pure humus, where one's eyes

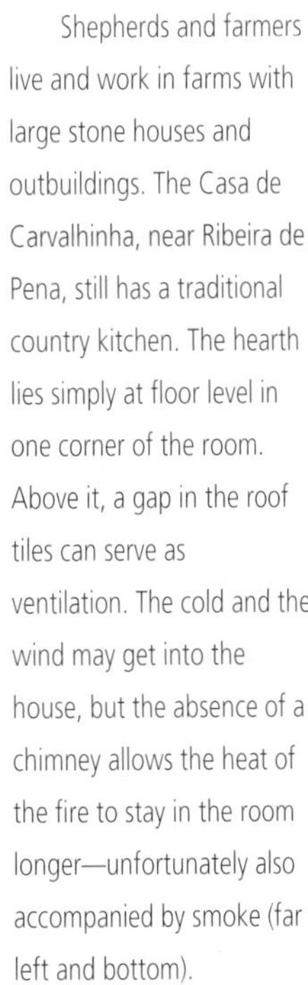

can rest awhile from the aggressiveness of rocks" (top).

These fertile valleys produce copious quantities of fruit and vegetables, as well as the rye which is used to produce an excellent round bread with a rich brown crust.

Shepherds and farmers live and work in farms with large stone houses and outbuildings. The Casa de Carvalhinha, near Ribeira de Pena, still has a traditional country kitchen. The hearth lies simply at floor level in one corner of the room. Above it, a gap in the roof tiles can serve as ventilation. The cold and the wind may get into the house, but the absence of a chimney allows the heat of the fire to stay in the room longer—unfortunately also accompanied by smoke (far left and bottom).

Here the vaulted wooden roof gives a greater sense of space in a bedroom with simple whitewashed walls on which hang groups of pictures and images of saints (right).

On the banks of the Lima a festival is in preparation. Soon this wooden scaffolding will be decorated with paper flowers and transformed into a triumphal arch to welcome the procession (top). In groups of four, the faithful will carry the *andores*—platforms displaying heavy wooden statues of saints dressed in gold-embroidered clothing.

The beauty of the river Lima was already appreciated in Roman times, when it was compared to Lethe, the river of forgetting. On its banks stands the amazing neo-Venetian palace of Portuzêlo, near Viana do Castelo (middle).

Estuaries are close to paradise—a cross between sea and land. The smell of the salty water mixes with that of the earth, birds swoop down, and light plays between sky and water. Ports were established here early on. Viana do Castelo functioned as a base for exporting wine and salt, and for importing cloth and the *bacalhau* (cod) that is so dear to the Portuguese (bottom and right).

The Douro threads its way between high, barely accessible mountains. Boats that once transported heavy barrels to Oporto have been replaced by the railway (left).

The station at Pinhão, a small town surrounded by mountains in the heart of this wine-producing territory, is famous for its azulejos. The tiled panels, created in 1937, depict Douro landscapes and scenes from the grape harvest (right).

A few moments rest, enjoying the warmth of a sunny corner (bottom).

QUINTAS AND GRAPEVINES

Northern Portugal is a land of traditions, traditions that are carved in granite, a difficult stone that the skills of sculptors have succeeded in metamorphosing into full, vibrant shapes. Throughout their history the inhabitants of the north have loved their schist and granite rocks. Even in the earliest days of settlement, it must have taken tremendous energy and expertise to build the terraces in the upper valleys of the Minho and the Douro.

Over the centuries, these stones have been turned into palaces and country homes—each with its own specific generic name. A *solar,* a word which is sometimes used incorrectly, can only mean a house or a place from which a family originated. A *honra* indicates that it once had important privileges. A *castelo* is a fortified castle, and a *palácio* is a residence of royalty or great size. A *paço* has been used as a residence by a king, an infanta, or one of the princes of the church, even if only for one night. The *casa* is a general term indicating anything from a simple house to a stately home, which is also called a *casa nobre* or *casa senhorial.* As for the term *quinta,* this refers to the land itself, often surrounded by walls, on which a house has been built.

In the valley of the Upper Douro, where the vineyards that produce port climb the hillsides, many of these houses are located within wine-producing *quintas.* The wine of this region already had a reputation when, in the seventeenth century, two Englishmen visiting a monastery near Lamego tasted a curious, sweet, velvety nectar. When they asked how it was made, the abbot told them the secret which was to become the basis of port: the addition of brandy during vinification. The merchants realized that this process would both assist in the ageing of the wine and facilitate its movement. Road transport to Viana do Castelo quickly gave way to a trip down the river Douro to Oporto, which was more accessible. This is why the wine born up here took the name *vinho do Porto.*

In the middle of the eighteenth century, the all-powerful marquis of Pombal created the Companhia Geral da Agricultura das Vinhas do

"On the banks of a golden river, crucified between the heat of the sky, which drinks it from above, and the thirst of its bed, which sucks it dry from beneath, rise the flanks of a miracle. On the stepped escarpments of terraces that belong to no palace, the vine stocks sprout like basil on balconies." Such was the Upper Douro for Miguel Torga (preceding double page and far right).

At the Quinta de Vargellas, the mountain, with its sculpted terraces, is bathed by the Douro's waters. The Robertsons enjoy entertaining and prepare excellent meals with their home-grown vegetables (bottom right). The terrace, shaded by a vine arbor, makes a pleasant place to taste the great Taylor's ports produced on the estate (top).

At the Quinta do Porto, a beautiful estate near Pinhão, Vito Olazabal, president of the Portuguese firm Ferreira, gives unforgettable dinners. Here one can taste a prestigious ten-year-old tawny—red, raisiny, and mellow—together with a *queijo da Serra*, a creamy, delicate ewe's milk cheese served with a slice of jellied quince (bottom left).

Alto Douro in order to regulate production and sale of the wine—almost exclusively to the British. Later it assigned the name to a defined territory, creating Europe's first demarcated region. It was not until the following century that wine merchants began to take a closer interest in the vineyards and started buying *quintas* in the Douro. There are now many of these *quintas,* testifying to the remarkable refinement of the wine masters.

THE QUINTA DE VARGELLAS. This handsome estate is one of the major *quintas.* It is located in the Upper Douro, an arid terrain where the river threads its way through a valley that seems inhospitable, but is actually excellent land for producing wine. In 1893 this renowned *quinta* was purchased by Taylor, the first English firm to buy land in the Douro. It soon became the jewel in the firm's crown, with wine from Vargellas providing the basis for Taylor's famous vintage ports.

It is a uniquely rewarding experience to arrive here on the picturesque little train from Oporto. Opposite Vargellas, the Douro flows into the lake of a dam, surrounded by vineyards on rising terraces dotted here and there with white houses. The train arrives in the tiny station of the *quinta,* where Alistair Robertson, Taylor's presiding genius, offers a warm welcome.

Oporto seems a world away. It is autumn, and the grape pickers are coming in from the surrounding countryside, sometimes to the tune of accordions or harmonicas. The creaking of ox carts can no longer be heard, but the mountain is still alive with a thousand sounds.

On all sides cohorts of men go up and down the stony paths and schist stairways leading to the terraces. Their wicker baskets are heavily laden with bunches of grapes with their characteristic royal blue tint. Picturesque images, tinged with the solemnity of this arduous labor, can be seen all through the year on the azulejos of the Pinhão station.

At the end of the day the wine-treading begins in the *lagares,* the large granite treading vats. Guests are invited to participate, as depicted in Willie Rushton's amusing drawings at Vargellas.

NOVAL

This method of treading the grapes is becoming less and less common, but it is still used in the Douro's more reputable *quintas* in order to produce the better vintage ports.

Near the *adega* (the storeroom) stands the stately white house with its Georgian-style colonnade and comfortable interior, decorated by the attentive hostess, Gillyane Robertson. Here one finds the English ambience so characteristic of the world of port. Gillyane recounts the beginnings, when they depended on the vegetable garden to supply their daily needs. Although they had no electricity, they always had plenty of visitors some even arriving by helicopter. Today's guests talk over their day and their impressions of Douro. It is hot and the Vargellas cocktail is delicious: white port, tonic water, and a mint leaf, accompanied by home-grown almonds and olives. The table is set on the shaded terrace as night gently falls.

The Quinta do Vesúvio. The memory of Dona Antónia Ferreira, a legendary figure in port, lives on in the Quinta do Vesúvio. Widowed in 1844 at the age of thirty-three, this remarkable woman turned her *quintas* into the best vineyards in the Douro. Her wealth and kindness won the admiration of her contemporaries, who called her the Ferreirinha. She was also the presiding spirit of the lovely Quinta do Porto, long owned by the Ferreira family and today belonging to the Sogrape group.

Dona Antónia turned the Quinta do Vesúvio—located high in the Upper Douro and spread across thirty-one valleys—into a "colossal, epic estate," as it was described by a nineteenth-century chronicler. The house, white and tall, with two floors and a baroque-style chapel, is impressive. Its façade and the small windows designed to keep out both heat and cold, blend perfectly into the environment—an amphitheater of mountains overlooking the Douro.

Before the railway was built in 1885, and the road in more recent times, the passage to Quinta do Vesúvio was by river. The small sailing boats that plied the Douro were the only link between the vineyards and Oporto downstream. The voyage of these *barcos rabelos,* laden with sixty barrels per boat, usually took three long days. For passengers the journey was often rough, due to the rapids and the fierce currents. The Symington group, which recently bought the Quinta do Vesúvio from the Ferreira family, is now attempting to run this prestigious vineyard along the lines of a Bordeaux château, producing "single ports" in which the grapes come from one sole *quinta.*

The Quinta do Noval. The Quinta do Noval is one of the most famous in the port wine industry. Already renowned in 1715, it later became the property of a family of merchants from Oporto, who put considerable effort into improving the vineyard's production. In the 1920s the terraces were redesigned, partly in order to extend the space available and partly to improve the exposure. Noval is a symbol of quality, which always takes pride of place over quantity, as exemplified in its single-port policy, and its particularly fine "vintages"—single ports produced exclusively from the grapes harvested in one particularly successful year.

At the Quinta do Noval there is an extraordinary contrast between the bluish shadow of the incredible eight-hundred-meter stretch of grapevines and the overwhelming panorama. The Douro, the terraces, everything is colored with the innumerable greens of the tree-like vines that overhang the manor. Here each season brings different fragrances. The whitewashed schist of the buildings gleams in the heat of the sun. Even the ridges of the brick roofs are immaculate. Tucked back against the slope, as always in the Douro region, the estate shelters not only the *adega* and the *armazém,* but also the chapel dedicated to Saint Nicholas, who has blessed so many a good harvest.

Looking out from the Quinta do Noval, it is hard to take one's eyes off the ocean of schist and grapevines, the impressive terraces built by the tenacity of men, the steeply rising mountains, and the river that flows deep in the valley (far left).

Noval is an oasis in the midst of the vineyards. At once a wine-producing estate and a comfortable residence, its elegance without ostentation is typically Portuguese (top).

An image of the charms of Portugal: 1990 vintage ports from the famous Quinta do Vesúvio, standing in front of a panel of blue-and-white azulejos. Until the middle of the eighteenth century, port bottles were pot-bellied with a long neck. Gradually they became more elongated, and by the middle of the nineteenth century the bottles had taken on their now classic shape (bottom).

Scrolled roofs, heraldic pediments, balustrades with ornamental statuary, and giant pinnacles rising into the Trás-os-Montes sky. This is the Casa de Mateus (left).

The interior lives up to the promise of the exterior. Here, handsome portières accentuate the series of doorways (top).

The administrators of the Casa de Mateus have always been men of culture. In 1817, one of them published Camões's *Lusiades*, with illustrations by Fragonard and Gérard. This monumental edition is preserved in the library (bottom).

Close to the house stands a kind of sanctuary, the famous Nacional estate, whose five thousand non-grafted grapevines escaped the tragic phylloxera outbreak which decimated the Douro region in 1868. Needless to say, the three thousand bottles of Nacional produced each year are a special treat reserved for true wine-lovers.

The Casa de Mateus. The art of living in Portugal is extraordinarily complex in its refinement. One of its finest splendors is the Casa de Mateus, near Vila Real, also known as the Solar de Mateus. The international reputation of this Portuguese palace is principally due to a wine. When Fernando Guedes was looking for a prestigious symbol for the rosé that he was creating, he asked the owner of the Casa de Mateus for permission to reproduce a picture of the palace on his labels. Now that the wine has become such a success, the Casa de Mateus continues to confer its prestige on an incalculable number of bottles.

Yet the reputation of Casa de Mateus would be ensured by its beauty alone, given that it is one of the most splendid baroque palaces in Europe. Its construction spanned a period from the seventeenth century to the middle of the eighteenth, and probably involved the Italian Nicolau Nasoni, a major Oporto architect. It is believed that Nasoni brought the dynamism to a structure that is otherwise fairly static, enlivening the courtyard with a staircase, balustrades, statues, pediments, and pinnacles. Nasoni is also credited with the typically baroque chiaroscuro effects, creating an interplay between the white of the walls and the golden gray of the stone. The talented Minho stonemasons brought life to this austere stone, adding to the palace's blend of nobility and exuberance that is so typically Portuguese.

In 1971, in an effort to preserve his family heritage and to make it available to the public, Dom Francisco de Sousa Botelho de Albuquerque set up the Casa de Mateus Foundation, which today is headed by his son,

At the Honra de Azevedo, every aspect of the building confers a sense of majesty. The wide upper gallery, with its regularly placed stone columns, faces south—offering shade in the summer and warmth in the cool season. The three arches on the ground floor, where the dining room is located, were only recently opened (top and bottom).

In this country where welcoming guests is always an art, the entry halls designed to receive visitors are often situated on the upper floor. Here the painted heraldic emblems at the center of the ceiling leave no doubt as to the social standing of the house's former owners. In a cartouche executed in rococo *trompe l'oeil* style, we see the flying eagle of the powerful Azevedo family. Wide benches with heraldic emblems and scrolled backs still stand in their original positions. The décor is completed by various *objets d'art*, turned-wood furniture, and embroidered Arraiolos carpets (right).

Dom Fernando. When speaking about his family's history, Dom Fernando explains that there has always been a powerful bond between the administrators of the estate—the *morgados*—and the Casa de Mateus. For each of them, both the palace and its land have been an obsession. This explains the vitality of the Foundation, which was created to preserve the Casa de Mateus and to organize a variety of cultural and scientific activities there.

Open to the public, the palace can be enjoyed to its fullest during music festivals, seminars, and literary events. A chamber music recital can provide a wonderful opportunity to admire the suite of rooms, with their magnificent carved-wood ceiling and the sumptuous family furniture. Not to be missed are the large painted-wood benches with carved backs and the impressive portières—embroidered felt doorway curtains bearing the family coat of arms.

Outside, the gardens bear witness to the family's long-standing efforts to maintain Casa de Mateus as a work of art. The dream image, the traditional postcard view, is of course the view of the palace suffused with a halo of light and reflected in the flower-edged ornamental pool. But another magical sight, in the tradition of baroque gardens, is the long tunnel of cedar trees, where the twisted, gnarled, serried ranks of tree trunks on the interior contrasts with the exterior, trimmed to resemble a twenty-foot-high caterpillar. The shadowy light continues under the immense vine arbor, its granite pillars sculpted in the shape of obelisks lending it a majestic presence. Nearby, the studied layout of box borders, the camellia garden, and the ornamental pools designed by the architect António Lino each have their own special charm.

THE HONRA DE AZEVEDO. This prestigious Minho castle, located near Barcelos, is another estate where wine is the dominant theme. The *solar* of the powerful Azevedos, which has been in the

same family for nearly eight hundred years, has been enlarged and redesigned over the centuries. It now belongs to Sogrape, the Portuguese firm which, in 1942, created Mateus Rosé, a sweet, slightly sparkling wine enjoyed throughout the world. Following in the footsteps of Fernando Guedes, the creator of Mateus Rosé, his son Fernando, with the aid of his wife Dona Mafalda, has been especially successful in bringing the castle back to life and giving it a warmth all its own.

The power of the imposing keep is somewhat softened by the presence of a broad, columned upper gallery looking out over the countryside, and by an arcaded patio where wisteria grows. Inside, on the ceiling of the main hall, the imperious eagle of the Azevedos, painted in a rococo cartouche, seems to watch over the house's visitors. Furniture, carpets, *objets d'art,* and even tiled panels contribute to the very Portuguese elegance of this *solar.* The kitchen is also typical of the Minho, with its salting tub, its ovens, and the huge granite hood supported on columns. Propitiously placed next to the hearth are two traditional wooden benches, known in local parlance as *preguiçeiros*—a good place to idle away an hour or two.

A WELCOME TO THE MANOR

This very particular ambience is also to be found in Minho's prestigious stately homes, which were built for the most part between the sixteenth and

In the park of the Honra de Azevedo, a combination of grapevines, wooded hills, and flourishing vegetation make up a truly Minhoto landscape (bottom).

Trees silhouetted in the mist, a curving red-tiled roof, ornamental stone vases, a magical doorway that must bear the arms of a very old family—this is the Casa de Sezim, near Guimarães. The splendid late-eighteenth-century doorway, with the coat of arms of the Freitas do Amaral family, is roughcast in a pink that is unusual for the region. An open door invites the traveler to enter and discover the charm of this manor house: the courtyard, the drawing rooms and bedrooms opening onto the garden, and the long terrace where time seems to stand still (right).

It was probably Manuel de Freitas do Amaral Castelo Branco, one of the forebears of the present owners, who chose this panoramic wallpaper for the Casa de Sezim. Here one sees the views of North America created by Jean Zuber in 1834 at Rixheim in Alsace. In the left foreground travelers are admiring the extraordinary Utah Arch, a naturally formed stone bridge. On the other side of the doorway, a boat steams along in front of the Niagara Falls. These panoramas were so successful that they were soon being ordered from all around Europe, and even from the United States (far right).

In this delightful house, which accepts paying guests, the dining room and the bedrooms are fitted out with elegant family furniture and East India Company porcelain (top and bottom).

nineteenth centuries and are still surrounded by working agricultural estates. These are mainly vineyards, producing various sought-after varieties of *vinho verde*, such as the famous *alvarinho* of Paço da Brejoeira, the excellent Casa de Sezim from near Guimarães, or Paço d'Anha from near Viana do Castelo. Visitors who came to taste these wines also developed a taste for the region, and gradually the owners of the houses have opened their doors to guests.

The formula of château-based residential tourism developed by the count of Calheiros and his fellow manor house owners in the north has struck a chord with tourists looking for new ways of visiting the country and has quickly spread to other parts of Portugal.

The success of this venture lies as much in the charm and comfort of the manor houses as in the warm hospitality and social standing of the people who live in them. It should be added that most of the château owners, being both polyglot and passionate about their Minho, are the best ambassadors the region could wish for. It has been known for visitors to return home, find themselves stricken with *saudade*, and then decide to learn Portuguese in order to read the captivating *Novelas do Minho*, which unfortunately have not been translated. Written by Camilo Castelo Branco, the Portuguese Balzac, these texts bring to life Minho society of the nineteenth century, and often make reference to the forebears of the people who act as hosts today. In fact, one of the attractions of a visit to the north is that many of the estates that welcome guests have been handed down through successive generations for over five hundred years.

The Casa de Sezim, near Guimarães, is one such estate that has been in the same family for several centuries. This pink-walled manor house, laid out in a U-shape, is entered via a traditional armorial gateway. António and Maria Francisca Pinto Mesquita, the warmest of hosts, receive their visitors in a series of large interlinking drawing rooms. The extraordinary nineteenth-century wallpaper, which was produced by the Mulhouse firm of Zuber, invites the mind to travel. There are two sets of images, showing views of North America and Hindustan, as well as a few panels of Napoleon Bonaparte's campaign in Egypt. The fresh colors of these delightful panoramas combine with the furniture and family portraits to create an atmosphere of warm elegance, while the bedrooms, located in a separate wing of the house, look out onto the tranquil gardens.

The region's manor houses always have something new, unusual and exciting in store. And this is precisely one of the attractions of the Minho. At Paço de Calheiros, the most striking feature is the turrets. This architectural feature—along with other characteristics such as a chapel located at the center of the house, and an upper gallery—seem to have been the inspiration for other manor houses in the region of Ponte de Lima. In the evening, when the scent of wisteria is at its strongest, it is delightful to look out from the turret over the valley of the Lima and to enjoy a cool drink while the count and countess of Calheiros talk about their region. Below, the grand stone staircase is extraordinary, in the manner of all Minho staircases. Always built on the outside of the building, and presenting an ever-changing aspect to the onlooker, they are above all the symbol of a welcome that is unstinting, and that comes from the heart.

There is, however, the story of another, more tragic welcome that remains engraved in local memory. This occurred at the Paço d'Anha, near Viana do Castelo. It was here that the pretender to the Portuguese throne, Dom António, the prior of Crato, took shelter in 1580 while he was being hunted by the Spaniards. Maria Augusta d'Alpuim, one of the present owners of Paço d'Anha, is writing a history of the region, and recounts the events that occurred within the house. She shows the seventeenth-century chapel, as well as the carefully preserved chest in which the unfortunate prince once hid. She also cheers the

Not far from Viana do Castelo, the picturesque Casa do Ameal has been handed down from generation to generation over several centuries, undergoing many transformations. The family has maintained a tradition of opening its doors to friends, and they now continue the practice with paying guests, who are always welcomed in style. The façade is mirrored in the huge granite ornamental pool with its baroque-style contoured edges (right).

The traveler who visits Minho is struck by the manor house turrets that suddenly appear from behind a line of trees or on a hillside. Sometimes from the top of a turret the colored flag of the lord of the manor flies in the breeze, for example, the flag of the Lancaster family at the Casa de Bertiandos near Ponte de Lima or that of the count of Águia at Torre d'Águia near Arcos de Valdevez.

These towers are usually emblematic, so that large windows and terraces replace the traditional narrow loopholes, as at Paço de Calheiros, an inviting country residence that is open to tourists (top and bottom).

visitor's heart by offering a glass of the estate's delicious Paço d'Anha *vinho verde*.

In each manor house, the history of Minho unravels like Ariadne's thread. At Paço de São Cipriano, near Guimarães, João and Maria Teresa de Sottomayor are always delighted to open their doors to visitors. Its complex layout is evidence of the interrelationship, created over several centuries, between a family and the walls that sheltered it. The interior has many of the typical surprises of château life—a superb granite kitchen, a medieval-style dining room, and bedrooms in the tower. Outside, the trimmed box hedges and the huge topiary cockerel in the tradition of English landscape gardening, are superb.

Quinta de Santa Comba near Barcelos, and Casa da Boa Viagem near Viana do Castelo, are both Minhoto marvels in which the majesty of a gateway and chapel go hand in hand with the good-humored charm of the adjoining manor. These gateways, erected in the eighteenth century, are one of the hallmarks of the *casas nobres* in Minho. Their heraldic pediments bear witness to the owner's seniority in a line of descent, to a social status that brings with it both duties and prerogatives, and to a desire to offer guests a fitting welcome.

At Boa Viagem, Júlia and José Teixeira de Queiroz share the pleasures of living in a such a house. In the park water spills into granite channels and funnels down into a monumental fountain that is roughcast in yellow ochre and where the cheerfulness of the granite statues is contagious. In the morning, the breakfast of home-made jam and lard bread is delicious.

Breakfast time is always a special moment in these manor houses. Often this meal is served in impressive granite kitchens, where the hearth and

The manor houses of Minho and Douro have been cherished by their owners for generations and contain furniture and objects that hold a thousand memories. At Paço d'Anha, a handsome guesthouse near Viana do Castelo, family collections were brought together by José de Alpuim da Silva de Sousa e Meneses, grandfather of the present owners. At Anha, which was his country house, travelers can now admire turned-wood beds, cabinets, precious glassware, and Chinese porcelain that reveal the collector's passion (top).

At Paço da Glória, everybody remembers the count of Santa Eulália. In the 1900s, thanks to the fortune of his American wife, he was able to transform this stately home into a fairy tale castle. Subsequently Lord Peter Pitt accentuated its romantic aspect, in the style of English country houses. Today, visitors who stay at this agreeable guesthouse particularly enjoy having their breakfast on the pleasant arcaded upper gallery (bottom).

Travelers once stopped at Paço de São Cipriano on their way to Santiago de Compostela. Tourists still come today, but this fabulous four-poster bed, worthy of the "Princess and the Pea," is considerably more comfortable than the rustic straw mattresses on which the pilgrims slept (right).

A chapel, topiary gardens, fountains, and external staircases are the basic elements of Minho's manor houses. At the Casa do Campo, the chapel, which appears very simple from the outside, opens onto a fabulous gold retable. In the gardens of this stately home, which is open to

paying guests, the camellias are trimmed like green sculptures, according to the rules of monumental topiary (left and above).

Water is ever-present in these gardens of the north. At the Quinta de Santa Comba, another delightful stopping-off point for the traveler, it splashes gently in a granite fountain (bottom right).

its ovens take up almost half of the available space. At Paço da Glória, near Arcos de Valdevez, the magnificent panorama from the wide arcaded upper gallery transforms breakfast into a moment of bliss. Here the *torradas* seem even tastier. These slices of thin white bread, toasted and drenched in salted butter, served as double-deckers and always cut in three, are a Portuguese specialty that should not be missed. Paço de Glória—recently restored by the present owner and art connoisseur, Maurício Macedo e Moreira—has an infinite, magical charm.

The gardens of Minho, and particularly those of the Basto region, are enchanting. This is the kingdom of camellias, the *japonicas* that took so easily to the Portuguese climate in the Age of Discoveries. The majestic Casa do Campo, near Celorico de Basto, where guests are received by

At the Casa da Boa Viagem, a very agreeable guesthouse, one can spend hours simply admiring the weathered stone of the fountain and the baroque sculptures of Chinese-style dragons and water gods. The staircase, echoing the one inside the house, is as much a symbol of social prestige as it is a means of circulation (top and bottom left).

Teixeira de Pascoaes's memory is kept alive at the Casa de Pascoaes, where the poet lived. Travelers who stay in the house can still admire his study (left).

The kitchen, with its granite table and columned hearth (right and bottom left), says everything about the art of living in Portugal—a country where people value hearty foods. A bowlful of *caldo verde*, a rustic cabbage soup, is still one of the symbols of the north (bottom right). Once the meal is finished, the wooden benches at the hearthside are an invitation to idleness.

Maria Armanda de Meireles, has the most amazing camellia garden in the whole of Portugal. This art of monumental topiary has been kept alive by the efforts of the country's château owners, of whom the hostess of Casa do Campo is a sterling example.

Pyramids, cylinders, arbors, and porticoes come together in a fascinating whole, which sometimes has an Egyptian air. From January to May, to drink an old Madeira here, sitting among spring flowers in the interplay of light and shadow beneath a covering of foliage, feels like a voyage to an unknown country. And the eighteenth-century chapel is resplendent with gold and carved woodwork.

The finest hymns to the beauty of the north, the cradle of the nation and the mythical location of a forgotten paradise, are incontestably those of the poet Teixeira de Pascoaes. His memory is scrupulously maintained in the house where he lived, the Casa de Pascoaes, near Amarante at São João de Gatão, (where Gatão *vinho verde* is produced). Here it was that the poet welcomed friends such as Unamuno and Raúl Brandão to reinvent the world. Maria Amélia Teixeira de Vasconcellos continues this tradition, offering guests from around the world the calm and coolness of her manor next to the river Tâmega.

In the large traditional kitchen one has an opportunity to taste the cuisine of the province that the poet so loved. A steaming *caldo verde* (traditional cabbage soup), together with a plate of *favas guisadas* (haricot beans) cooked with Trás-os-Montes ham and *chouriço,* is a meal fit for a king. The *vinho verde* of Amarante, a fruity wine, is a particularly fine accompaniment for these rustic dishes.

Oporto

Sunlight and shadow in the Bolhão market, where the harmonious architecture brings together iron and slate. The first-floor gallery resembles an opera set with crowds of extras, where the shouting and laughing and the hubbub of conversation mingle with a thousand aromas (preceding double page).

A gray city, Oporto? Just visit praça da Ribeira. Its polychrome façades make it one of the brightest and most picturesque spots in town. In their tight ranks, these houses illustrate the passion for ceramics. While the tile-covered façades look as if they have always been part of the landscape, the fashion actually dates from the nineteenth century. It was the Brazilians who discovered the thermal and technical qualities of glazed tiles, which until then had usually been reserved for interiors. This vogue then crossed the Atlantic and became the rage in Portugal (left).

The people of Oporto have a passion for metalwork. Wrought-iron railings running along from one house to another can be seen throughout the city (top).

Oporto has more than one "Eiffel Tower lying on its side" in the words of Paul Morand. The best known is the Dona Maria Pia bridge built by Gustave Eiffel. The Dom Luís bridge, inspired by this latter, was built further downstream in the 1880s. This boldly conceived iron arch straddles the river at a height of over two hundred feet to link Oporto with Vila Nova de Gaia (above).

Here glazed tiles reach even up to the chimneys (top).

Travelers can discover an exceptional azulejo façade on the church of dos Congregados, one of the finest in Oporto. The panels created by Jorge Colaço recount the life of Saint Anthony (bottom).

In the immense waiting room at the São Bento railway station, the azulejos tell the story of major incidents in Portugal's history and depict daily life in the provinces of Minho and Douro. Here, in 1916, the painter Jorge Colaço was perhaps trying to show that the certainties of the past could help to overcome the uncertainties of a present clouded by the assassination of the king, Dom Carlos and the difficult beginnings of the Republic (far right).

Early in the morning the train moves slowly across the Dona Maria Pia bridge, overlooking the dark waters of the river Douro. Suddenly, a city comes into view, clinging to the hillside—a city that has given its name to one of the finest wines in the world. Oporto is suffused with light. Everyone on the train falls silent, even those accustomed to the sight are fascinated by the ever-changing beauty of this apparition. Could this town be as gray and drab as its reputation? Or is that simply a rumor spread by promoters of the standard postcard Portugal, consisting of nothing but sun-drenched white houses?

Already a town in Roman times, Oporto grew up around the Pena Ventosa, a hilltop lashed by west winds where the cathedral now stands some two hundred feet above the river. From here narrow streets swarm down to the Douro—rua Senhora das Verdades, rua dos Mercadores—each a veritable sculpture, a living museum. Stairways, covered walkways, and alleys thread their way between dark houses for the most part constucted in depth so that they almost seem to be part of the hill itself. This lively, working-class neighborhood is a good example of the deep ties that still unite the city's residents. At the bottom of the hill lies the Ribeira, the riverfront area. Its houses and arcaded passages are buzzing with activity, recalling that the Douro was a major trade center until the artificial ocean port of Leixões was built some hundred years ago.

Today the heart of the city is being reborn under the guidance of the architect Fernando Távora. Its colors—yellow-ochre washes, blue azulejos, and polychrome glazed bricks—dulled by the years, are being restored. A sharp eye will also note that any color in this northern city is always softened by the slight mist and the pearl-gray light that permeate the atmosphere.

Oporto does not reveal itself at first glance. The vogue for exteriors covered in patterned tiles dates only from the nineteenth century, and originated in Brazil—a second country for emigrants from northern Portugal. The style was such a success that soon both new and old façades were covered by ceramics. The praça da Ribeira is a synthesis of this multicolored Oporto. Here white and yellow washes harmonize with blue or red glazed bricks and azulejos in shades of blue and white with patterns.

The façades in this audacious city are enticing and always full of life. On rua das Flores, one of the best examples of Oporto's eighteenth-century urban architecture, the tightly packed houses tend to be tall and narrow. Large windows occupy nearly the entire façade, providing an entry point for a silvery light, softened by the moisture-laden sea air. In some cases, as in praça Almeida Garret, the wall itself practically disappears. The golden-gray of the stone blends into the wrought-iron balcony railings that stretch along the house fronts. These balustrades are found everywhere—the city has a long tradition of metalworking and in Oporto traditions die hard.

One of the most impressive images of Oporto, the extraordinary Dona Maria Pia bridge, has inspired many a poet. It was "Brussels lace" for Teixeira de Pascoaes, and an "Eiffel Tower lying on its side" for Paul Morand. This unique arch, conceived by Gustave Eiffel in 1876, was the first of its kind in the world. It was later taken by one of his disciples as a model for the Dom Luís bridge further downstream. At the time, wrought iron was giving way to cast iron and steel, materials with new possibilities that were being enthusiastically explored. Since Oporto was always a city open to modernity, the new technology soon led to the building of splendid metallic structures. Sometimes simple, sometimes complex, often elaborately patterned, metalwork covered markets halls and invaded balustrades, doorways, and grilles. It even took over the roofs of houses, as an edging for the glass of innumerable *clara boias,* the wonderful skylights that sparkle in the sunlight by day and are transformed into magic lanterns by night.

The history of Portugal is written on Oporto's walls. During the early twentieth century—in a fervor tinged with the irrepressible yearning of *saudade*—architects, painters, and ceramists reinvented the large panels that had been fashionable in the eighteenth century. The most spectacular of these azulejos are undoubtedly the ones in the waiting room of the São Bento railway station, dating from 1916. The upper panel features a polychrome fresco illustrating the history of transportation, from the ox cart to the locomotive. Elsewhere, heroic pages of Portuguese history sit side by side with charming bucolic scenes depicted in varying hues of blue and white. Each is an invitation to board the poetic little train that climbs through the picturesque vineyards of Minho and Douro.

In the wake of this monumental project designed by Jorge Colaço—who also created the azulejos for the Buçaco Palace Hotel—other monuments, baroque and contemporary, were decorated with ornamental tilework. One of the pleasures of Oporto is to stroll about the town discovering churches where silver-gray sculpted granite ornaments commune harmoniously with these superb light-reflecting panels. On the walls of the dos Congregados, do Carmo, and das Almas churches, the azulejos recount the lives of the saints, in the preaching style of the pilgrimages known as *romarias*. The beauty of their deep blue tones is yet another reminder that the gray stones of Oporto always resound with color.

On the steeply rising shore of the Douro—the river of gold—stands the *cicade invicta*, the old and unconquered city, free and proud. It is the end of the day and the last rays of sunlight illuminate the imposing cathedral that dominates the city's church towers, wealthy residences, and humble houses in a harmony of blue-gray, ochre, and white (following double page).

In 1914, the architect Correia da Silva rebuilt the Bolhão market, which had already been a part of the city's center for several decades. He planned a two-level structure using the metalwork which was so much in vogue at the time. Partly open to the sky, awnings and shades protect the stalls from the vagaries of the weather (top, middle, and far right).

Surrounded as it is by a prosperous countryside, Oporto has always had lively, well-attended markets. This tradition of conviviality is closely linked to that of religious festivals, an essential element in the culture of the north. Fruits and vegetables are piled up on stalls, and may be sliced for the customer on the spot (bottom).

EVERYDAY LIFE IN OPORTO

The pulse of Oporto can be taken at the Bolhão market, established in an immense metalwork structure. According to Eduardo Paz Barroso in *A Taste of Oporto,* such "traditional markets offer a fine opportunity to discover Oporto's deeply Latin and southern temperament, which is normally hidden beneath an Atlantic restraint. The smell of tripe and blood sausage—an indispensable part of Oporto's gastronomic culture—the cackling of poultry, the sight of fish laid out on marble slabs, the incessant comings and goings of a bustling crowd of market women carrying baskets bulging with fruit, vegetables, and scented flowers among customers looking for bargains—all this is a sign of the vitality of this city that has been able to maintain at its heart the simplest, almost archaic, forms of a sensitive and tasteful relationship with everyday life."

While rustic recipes based on cooked blood are very much part of Oporto's tradition, its best-known specialty is tripe. This fare is so tied to the town's history, that its citizens are often referred to as *tripeiros* (tripe-eaters). Everywhere, from upscale restaurants to the humblest neighborhood *tasca,* it is a point of honor to cook the finest tripe dishes. One of the best is *tripas a moda do Porto,* garnished with pork, sausage, and chicken, and served with haricot beans.

Until a few decades ago, the Ribeira open-air market was primarily provisioned by boats coming down the river Douro. Today, although much

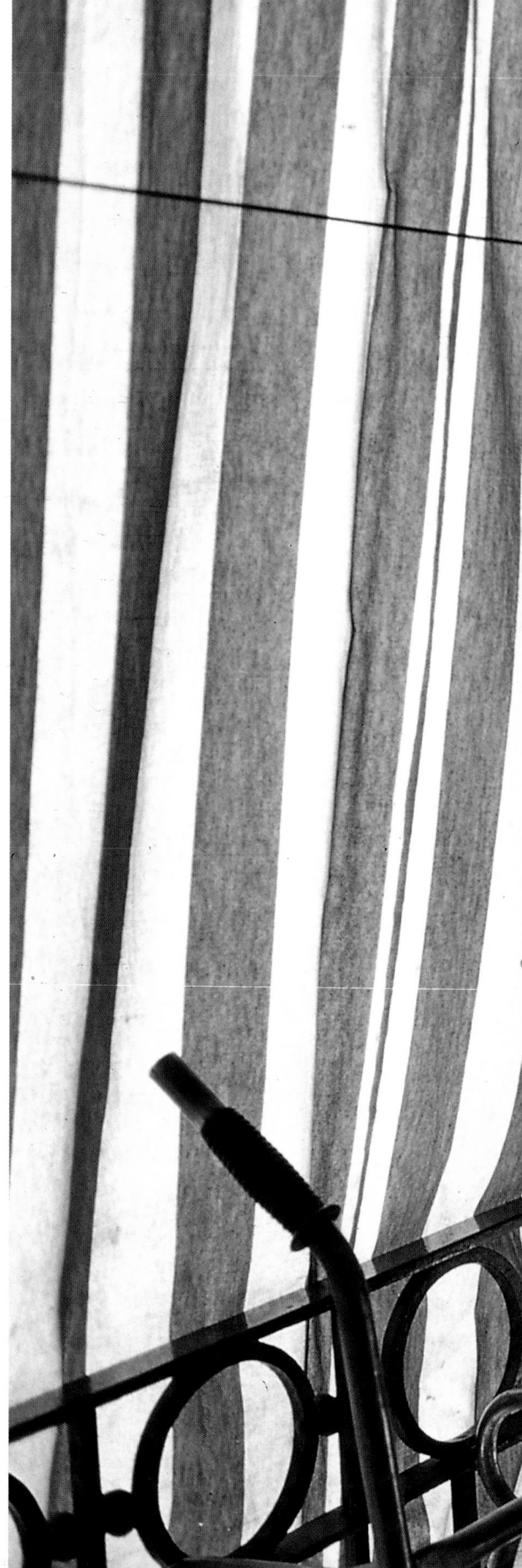

On the Ribeira riverside, the Taverna do Bebodos has been welcoming clients since 1876, as its sign proudly proclaims (top left). In the charming dining room that looks out over the river Douro a rustic regional cuisine can be savored. One house specialty is *papas de sarrabulho,* a soup that José Saramago has made famous, and which, according to him, "feeds the body and delights the soul" (middle left).

The north has been cod country since the end of the fifteenth century when it was first brought back by hardy sailors navigating in the cold, distant, fish-filled waters off the coast of Newfoundland. That was the start of a long relationship between the Portuguese and their *bacalhau*—sometimes known as the *fiel amigo*, the "faithful friend." In Oporto the Casa Oriental (bottom left and right) is a must for lovers of salt cod. The fish are displayed in the storefront like works of art.

The riverside is also the location for the Ribeira market. Originally produce was brought by boat both from the coast and inland. The appetizing foods still being offered include this corn bread (top right) which is so much a part of Portuguese cuisine. Jorge Tavares da Silva, an ethnologist and gastronome, explains how bread is to be found everywhere: in the *açordas* (soups), *migas* (sauces), *ensopados* (stews), in certain delicatessen meats—*alheiras* —and in the various recipes for *fatias*—delicious sugary slices of French toast.

On the façade of A Pérola do Bolhão, facing the entrance of the Bolhão market, two young women, looking like something out of some exotic opera, are painted on azulejos. In Portugal, as in China, tea is called *chá* (right).

The merchant who presides in this handsome imitation marble décor near the Bolhão market offers advice to his customers, and sells them seeds in multicolored sachets, or from canvas sacks on the floor (far right).

of the produce is trucked in, the market still provides all that is needed to prepare everyday Portuguese dishes. Piled on wooden trestles on the embankment are onions, potatoes, and Galician cabbage, which can be bought thinly sliced on the spot to prepare *caldo verde*. This characteristic northern Portuguese soup is made with the addition of a dash of olive oil and a slice of *chouriço* sausage. Further on are the breads that traditionally accompany Portuguese soups, such as the *broa de milho,* an exquisite corn bread with a yellowish color and a thick, crunchy crust. Other stalls sell fish, and, of course, salt cod in particular.

What is the best way to cook salt cod? This is one of the secrets of the Portuguese, who instinctively know how to impart sophistication to the simplest of materials. In the same way that humble clay can be metamorphosed into intricate azulejos, this plain fish can be prepared in a different manner for each day of the year. Originally a staple of working-class meals with their traditional family recipes, salt cod has gradually been adopted by

Portuguese society in general and recipes are passed down from one generation to another in even the highest echelons of society.

Among these innumerable creations, the *bacalhau à Brás,* a daring mix of cod, mashed potatoes, and eggs, is a wonderful delicacy. A more rustic offering, the inescapable codfish croquettes—*pastéis de bacalhau*—are eaten cold at the counters of bars and popular *tascas,* or hot, at home, with rice or salad. Not to be missed is the *bacalhau à Margarida da Praça,* a specialty of Viana do Castelo, one of the first towns in Portugal to have developed salt-cod fishing.

While all regions of Portugal have their own ways of cooking *bacalhau,* Ribeira is the birthplace of one of the most famous recipes, the *bacalhau à Gomes de Sá,* a dish which takes its name from a fishmonger who sold cod in the city nearly a hundred years ago. It consists of cod, garlic, onion, olives, eggs, and potatoes, and is truly a delight. Other local recipes, such as *bacalhau à Zé do Pipo, bacalhau à congregado,* or *arroz de bacalhau* come to mind when window-shopping at the Casa Oriental near the Torre dos Clerigos. The front of this colorful grocery store presents an artistic display of white dried cod tinged with gold. Carefully arranged, stacked, or hung with pride, the cod no longer resembles fish at all and becomes more than just food.

There are several traditional shops still operating in Oporto and their carefully maintained old-world surroundings are a delight. Tea and coffee can be purchased at the Chávena de Ouro or the Pérola da Guiné (the Pearl of Guinea), where the décor evokes memories of Portugal's empire. Traditional dried fruits and smoked delicatessen meats are available at the Pérola do Bolhão with its *Belle Époque* façade.

In the Confeitaria Império, a traditional Oporto pastry shop located on a busy shopping street, one can try delicacies made with egg yolk and featuring colorful names such as the famous *charutos d'ovos* (egg cigars), *jesuitas* (puff-pastry

The Portuguese love their cakes and sweets. The Casa Margaridense sells the traditional Easter crown, the *pão de ló,* a moist sponge cake (bottom left). Here one also finds *marmeladas,* the jellied quince that Portuguese housewives make in the autumn, and which is then left to dry in porcelain bowls during the winter months. Placed at the top of a cupboard, they give off a delicate scent (left).

The Portuguese are happy to spend time in a pastry shop. A small coffee is always welcome, together with an *império,* a puff-pastry that is a specialty of the Confeitaria Império (bottom right).

cakes), and even *Napoleões* (chocolate-filled flaked pastry). The Casa Margaridense sells a delicious *pão de ló,* a moist wheel-shaped sponge cake eaten mainly at Easter. Gourmets serve it with a portion of jellied quince and a glass of port. A Christmas specialty is the *bolo Rei,* a delicious puff-pastry ring decorated with candied fruits that has a tiny charm hidden inside. Another well-known dessert is the *pudim Abade de Priscos,* a delicacy consisting of eggs, sugar, lemon, port, and cinnamon, created by Father Rebelo, a leading church figure of Braga and a well-known gastronome. Having savored all these delights, a visit to Lello & Irmão should not be missed. This bookstore is located in a remarkable neo-Gothic building dating from 1906. Surrounded by ornately carved woodwork, the books take on an almost sacred quality.

As for the Casa de Serralves, featuring 1930s architecture, it was built for the count of Vizela, Carlos Alberto Cabral, an industrialist who was also a devotee of the latest artistic movements. At least part of

The name A Pérola da Guiné (the Pearl of Guinea) awakens nostalgic memories of a land that was discovered by the Portuguese in 1446. Inside, the tiles depict a plantation in Africa and a tea ceremony in China. In a cartouche the shop's motto is spelled out with a certain solemnity: "The best coffee and the best tea are those of the Pearl of Guinea" (top).

the building was designed by the Oporto architect Marques da Silva. In this pink palace, the organization of space is conceived in a new way. Inside, stucco, a common feature in northern Portugal, is reinvented in the form of long, slender fluting which spreads across the walls like musical waves. Furniture was chosen by the count himself from the finest Parisian studios such as Ruhlmann, Subes, Brandt, and Lalique.

Conceived within the same aesthetic, the surrounding park, which extends directly out from the palace, is a perfect place for the leisurely walks much appreciated by *portuenses*. In the gardens—laid out by Jacques Greber, a Frenchman who did extensive work in America—recollections of California mingle harmoniously with a French landscaping tradition. The park holds a host of surprises such as an idyllic lake, a meadow complete with sheep, and a small tearoom. The entire premises, now the property of the state, are maintained as a foundation open to the public and dedicated to contemporary art.

An agreeable restaurant on the Ribeira is the Mercearia. People love its warm ambience—granite walls, azulejos, exposed beams, and, of course, the view over the Douro (right).

In some Oporto shops artisanal soaps, very much in demand, are still cut to order (bottom).

Lello & Irmão, established in 1881, is one of Oporto's most prominent bookstores. This extraordinary building, commissioned in 1906, seems to be inspired by the Gothic cathedrals and fantastic castle libraries from some mythical England (far right).

The Casa Serralves was finished in the 1930s by Marques da Silva, a leading Oporto architect, for Carlos Alberto Cabral. A rich textile industrialist, Cabral made frequent visits to Paris, which he admired for its rich cultural life. All the classicism of Art Deco is found in its purity of line. The count of Vizela bought from the best studios in Paris in order to furnish this pink palace, which, with its interplay of volumes, is suggestive of a Palladian villa. Furniture came from Jacques-Emile Ruhlmann, wrought ironwork from Edgar Brandt and Raymond Subes, glass objects from René Lalique. Although a lot of the furniture and fittings have now disappeared, some fine examples still remain, such as this ornate metal grille (top).

Carlos Alberto Cabral paid particular attention to the gardens, which were designed with the help of a French landscape artist. The work began in 1932 and continued until 1940. In front of the palace, the symmetrical garden—defined by box hedges, ornamental pools, waterfalls and clumps of flowers—only seems to be classical (facing page). Further on, as the garden approaches the Douro, it is more freely landscaped, with a delightful romantic lake, a rose garden, a meadow with grazing sheep, and even a charming tearoom tucked away beneath the wisteria.

Located in an old Art Deco villa, the Casa do Marechal is one of Oporto's more charming hotels (bottom).

These long wine storehouses with their red-tiled roofs lie along the bank of the Douro or climb the hill of Vila Nova de Gaia (left). It was argued that the wines benefited from the air here, which was more humid than that of their birthplace in the hot valley of the Douro. In addition, the law stipulated that all port wines were to be matured and bottled at Vila Nova de Gaia. The law has since been changed, the art of air conditioning has progressed, and Noval, for example, has been shifting its wine storehouses to the Douro.

Sometime between 1920 and 1930 Adriano Ramos-Pinto commissioned this famous label from the distinguished Parisian poster designer René Vincent (bottom).

MASTERS OF PORT

The city's west side, which became fashionable in the 1930s, had long been a favorite of the English colony in Oporto. In *An English Family,* the writer Júlio Dinis describes the three "regions" of nineteenth-century Oporto: the center, Portuguese, the east, Brazilian, the west, English, with its simple, elegant, color-washed residences and gardens full of flowers. An excellent example is a house with gardens overlooking the Douro that formerly belonged to an English family and is now occupied by the novelist Agustina Bessa Luís. One of the leading lights of contemporary Portuguese literature, she often writes about the English in Oporto, as in her widely read novel *Fanny Owen.*

Throughout the history of Portugal, the alliance with the British has been viewed as a counterweight to the country's powerful Spanish neighbor. These privileged relations led to the development of trade in the traditional wines of Douro, the *maduros,* which had long been greatly appreciated in Britain. Exports increased in the seventeenth century, when the practice developed of adding brandy to stop fermentation, thus giving rise to *generosos,* or port wines. This operation, called "mutage," retains the sugar, giving port its smooth, velvety texture. It also improves the ageing process, making it easier to store and transport the wine.

During the eighteenth and nineteenth centuries the English wine traders in Oporto were not much interested in cultivating vineyards or in the actual production of the wine. They were concerned with the barrels of wine brought down the Douro on flat-bottomed *barcos rabelos* as far as Vila Nova de Gaia—the town facing

The storehouses or lodges, and the wine that ages in them, are the object of constant care (below, the Ramos-Pinto winery).

It is well worth a visit to the storehouses, where the wine is left to age for an average of three years, or, in the case of some tawnies, for more than forty years.

Oporto from the other side of the river. Later, the barrels were carried by train, and today they arrive by truck. Along the hillside stand the wine storehouses or lodges with red-tiled roofs, on which are painted the names of various firms. The storehouses hold the precious bottles, oak barrels, and enormous casks called "tuns," which can contain up to one hundred thousand liters each. It is here, in the half light of the lodges, that ports are created.

The appellation "port" covers an extraordinary complexity of wines. They may be blended or not, and may come from one single *quinta* or from several vineyards. The types of grapevine may differ, and the harvests chosen may date from the same year, or may be spread over several decades. Ageing takes place in oak casks and in bottles, and is the longest maturation process required for any wine. Obviously this alchemist's work requires a prodigious memory and an understanding of the maturing and equilibrium of wines. The masters of these wineries must have an extraordinary talent and sense of refinement to be able to create ports true to the spirit of their respective labels.

Vintage ports are the most sought after ports on the English market. These wines are produced from the grape harvests of one single estate, or even from the best plots on those estates. In addition, they are produced from a single particularly successful year or "vintage." After several months of ageing in barrels, the wine is bottled, and is then stored for fifteen to twenty years before being con-

After many years of use, the oak of worn barrels is sometimes used to make paving slabs for wine storehouses. Vintage ports age for a short period in barrels or casks, and are then transferred to bottles. They have a fruity taste and a remarkable heady bouquet. A visit to a lodge, which is always followed by a wine tasting, has a liturgical air about it (top and bottom, the Taylor winery).

Color, fragrance, and taste combine to create in port a sublime nectar that must be tasted according to the precise rules of the art. The traditional tulip-shaped glass enables the wine's bouquet to be liberated. This one bears an emu, the remarkable bird emblem of the Ferreira firm, which has been producing ports of great subtlety for nearly two hundred and fifty years (top).

Durability and tradition are the watchwords of the Ramos-Pinto company, which has kept its offices in the style created in 1908 by its founder, Adriano Ramos-Pinto (far right).

A number of well-known people have chosen to live in Oporto, including the architects Alvaro Siza Vieira and Fernando Távora, the film-maker Manoel de Oliveira and the novelist Agustina Bessa Luís. Miguel Veiga (bottom), a lawyer and leading figure in liberal politics is very active in the city's affairs.

sumed. Among the best are Dow's, Graham, Noval, Taylor, and Warre.

The tawnies are the true classics of port. These amazingly complex wines are often blends of several harvests, and may be left to age in casks for several decades. Moreover, the evaporation is regularly compensated for by the addition of more recent vintages. Portuguese firms, Ferreira and Ramos-Pinto for example, have traditionally excelled in the passionate alchemy of producing tawnies, which they rightly treat as works of art. This is unquestionably one of the finest examples of the Portuguese way of life.

Other ports must also be discovered: the whites, which are fruity and make perfect aperitifs, the young, engaging rubys, and the late-bottled vintages, which can be served during the course of a meal, with cheese, or even dessert. The tasting of a vintage port or an old tawny is a splendid moment! To appreciate them at their best they should be savored only after the meal.

Where better to taste and buy these wines than at Vila Nova de Gaia? Among the many local wineries, the firm of Ferreira is one of the most prestigious. The storehouses of this leading Portuguese winery, founded in 1751, are spectacular. It is one of the few to have preserved samples of all its vintage ports since 1830.

The Portuguese firm Ramos-Pinto specializes in the sale of port wines to Brazil. The firm was founded by Adriano Ramos-Pinto, who, as art-lover himself, understood that wine is a cultural product. At the end of the nineteenth century he commissioned well-known graphic artists to design his labels and decorated the company's premises with modern-style azulejos. Another magical spot, the superb Taylor winery, is also a must. Like darkened cathedrals these storehouses guard precious oak barrels that gleam slightly in the dim light.

The world of port can also be explored at the Solar do Vinho do Porto, where more than two hundred and fifty wines are available for tasting and are served with traditional grilled almonds. A brilliant alliance of two nations has enabled the creation of these complex wines that blend strength with a smooth sweetness.

Would this fantastic adventure ever have seen the light of day were it not for the traditional hospitality and acceptance of the Portuguese? The English, who still play an important role in Oporto society, have left their stamp on the city's culture. In trying to recreate their own world everywhere, they have influenced Oporto's way of life. The palatial Feitoria Inglesa, where British wine traders have conducted their affairs for over two hundred years, is a good example. A grandiose building, designed by a prestigious English architect at the end of the eighteenth century, it still houses the venerable club where twelve British firms, the "British houses," are represented. Wednesday lunch, at which the members of these firms meet, is a veritable institution. Anyone who is anyone in Oporto remembers having at one time or another danced in the splendid ballroom, beneath its crystal chandeliers.

The tradition of English clubs was also taken up in Oporto. The Ateneu Comercial do Porto, for example, a meeting place for the mercantile upper class, was founded in the middle of the nineteenth century. The solemnity of its many-flighted staircase, the goldwork and columns of the ballroom, the salons, and the library all illustrate the certainties and prodigious dynamism of triumphant capitalism confident in the infinite progress of humanity.

The Club Portuense, another locale where Oporto's high society gathers, is a product of the monarchist tradition very much a part of life in the north. The furniture, the frescoes, and the stuccoes all recall the atmosphere of Portugal's refined family houses. This very private club is an inviting place to settle in and forget the bustle of the city while savoring an exquisitely prepared fish or a luscious dessert, reminiscent of the delicacies prepared by the chefs of stately homes.

The Methuen Treaty, which was signed in 1703 to establish favorable trading relations between Britain and Portugal, explains much about the Portuguese way of life. In exchange for its wines, the Portuguese market was opened to English products. From that point onward, all sorts of links developed between the two countries. In Oporto, as they were accustomed to do throughout the world, the English merchants soon set up a "British Association," and established a commercial syndicate which was known as the Feitoria Inglesa. To house it, the architect John Whitehead built a prestigious neoclassical building which provides an image of the power of the British in Oporto. A showcase of English culture, it is impressive for its Palladian main hall, the wealth of its library, and above all its immense salons, which for more than two centuries have witnessed the comings and goings of Oporto's high society (top left).

Many superb meals have been prepared in the kitchens of the Feitoria Inglesa. Here one sees molds which, according to the institution's archives, were brought over from England (top right and bottom).

The English club tradition is still very much alive in Oporto. The Club Portuense, established in 1910 shortly before the fall of the monarchy, is the most elegant in Oporto. Admission is granted only by recommendation and after a vote by existing members. The monumental main hall, the salons, and the library are exquisitely furnished. Coming out parties are given here for debutantes, the daughters of Oporto's leading families (far right).

On the road South

From Aveiro to Óbidos, via Coimbra and the Ribatejo

The provinces of Beira Alta, Beira Baixa, and Beira Litoral in central Portugal, for Miguel Torga, were simply an emanation of the imposing Serra da Estrêla, "a sort of granite matrix" rising to a height of over 6,000 feet and Portugal's highest mountain range. Even when passing through the Beira Litoral, which borders the ocean, the foothills of the Serra da Estrêla are never far away. The rivers Alva and Mondego, originating in the mountains, are a constant reminder of the rocky interiors. The most natural route south passes through this amazing province of contrasts—mountains and plains, wide valleys and broad estuaries, all opening onto the low-lying coastline.

Miguel Torga adds that the entire coastal strip should form a province unto itself: "This long, pale fringe of lace edging the motley colors of the Lusitanian blanket. . . . The Atlantic, always the beach and . . . the fishermen. Always a wave dashing at the bow of a small boat laden with men waiting for a break in the waves so as to put out to sea." Given that natural shelters are rare along the Atlantic coast, this type of picturesque but dangerous fishing is dying out. However, around Aveiro, at Furadouro, and Torreira in the north, and at Mira in the south, there are still fishermen who join forces to haul their boats and nets up onto the beach with teams of oxen that plough through chest-deep water.

These beaches that seem to extend forever are exquisitely beautiful, wild, tinged with mystery, and often bathed in a silvery, pearly light. Many vacationers come here specially for the coast's combination of golden sands and bracing waves that are kept coming—even in the summer—by cold currents and strong ocean winds.

In the north, near Aveiro, an offshore bar nearly thirty miles long creates an extended estuary known as a *ria*. Vaguely defined, almost formless, it is shaped by mists, the golden evening light, the ocean haze, and the heat of the earth. Here fresh water and sea water mix around sand, salt pans, and fields. Reeds and pine forests make it the realm of wild ducks and fishermen. Sometimes huge, flat-bottomed boats called *moliceiros* can still be seen sailing across the lagoon, with raised prows and sails billowing in the wind. The collective memory has forgotten the origins of the extraordinary crescent-shaped prows, but tradition requires that owners pay particular attention to their boats' decoration. The sides are painted in wildly exuberant colors and a naive style with historical events, scenes from everyday life and proverbs, or with images of the Virgin Mary, patron saints, and famous people.

The river Mondego is far more peaceful. A symbolic river, it was long the frontier between the crosses of Portuguese kings to the north and the crescents of Moors to the south. Many of the country's poets have sung the river's praises—the surrounding countryside is so incomparably gentle it is bound to inspire lyricism. Verdant hills, fertile fields, soft green rice fields, and bountiful orchards surround the meandering course of the Mondego, bordered by willows and poplars. An abundance of trees punctuating the

The sylvan forest of Buçaco is one of the finest in Europe, at once mysterious and enchanting, as several hundred native Iberian species intermingle with nearly three hundred exotic ones. Roads and paths pass through the midst of its tall trees, where springs and waterfalls murmur among ferns and greenery. It is almost a sacred place, and is in fact protected by a papal bull of 1643. The palace hotel, with its turrets and pinnacles, appears like some strange plant springing out of the swell of verdure (preceding double page).

A few miles further on lies the sea and its beaches such as Praia da Vagueira (below) where remarkable chapels sometimes stand. These pilgrimage sites at times also serve as landmarks for sailors. Here we see the capela do Senhor da Pedra, near Miramar. A celebrated pilgrimage once took place here during the month of May (far left).

On the Aveiro lagoon, which sometimes resembles a Japanese landscape, handsome flat-bottomed boats called *moliços* sail slowly through the mist (following double page).

Horizontal lines of sand and water are found everywhere—the coast, the *ria*, the offshore bar, and the sea itself. But here in Costa Nova the lines are all vertical: multicolored planks of wood

stripe the façades of fishermen's houses called *palheiros*, while faïence tiles adorn more modern buildings. The ingenuousness of this architecture has always been captivating (top left, middle, and right).

The men of this region are simultaneously sailors and peasants, as might be expected, given that they live on the estuary or *ria*. They use their boats, decorated in bright colors, to transport salt, to fish for eel, and to harvest the seaweed intended to fertilize the land (bottom).

landscape are one of the great riches of Portugal. The forest climbs to the heights, covers the hills, and rolls down to the plains, while a heady aromatic scent of eucalyptus mingled with pines is carried by the winds to distant parts. This scent is particularly noticeable south of Coimbra, in the legendary pine forest of Leiria, planted in the Middle Ages by the monks of Alcobaça in order to stabilize shifting coastal sandbanks.

This forest, a paradigm of the eternal rivalry of man with his natural allies of earth and water, provides an example of how the country has gradually been shaped by the human hand. Another illustration of man's domination of nature is the province of Ribatejo—on the bank of the Tagus. Over the centuries this wide-spanning alluvial terrain has also contributed to the wealth of Portugal. However, the river often overflows, mingling with tidal waters that reach up to thirty miles inland. During such major flooding, the sight of meadows covered with a sheen of water gleaming in the sun can take on an almost cosmic aspect. Suddenly the mysterious fusion of the four elements—earth, water, the fire of the sun and the transparent air—seems almost possible.

On the right bank of the river the landscape is already suggestive of the neighboring Estremadura province. While on the left bank, huge estates of wheat, and occasionally rice, grapevines, and olives, spread across the vast plain. But Ribatejo is most often associated with the huge expanses of lush grassland, the *lezírias,* that provide grazing grounds for herds of cattle and horses, as well as black bulls destined for the ring. Working in the same way as herdsmen of the French Camargue and gauchos of Argentine pampas, the *campinos,* on their small, lively, nervous horses, keep watch over the animals using a long goad—the *pampilho.* A sensation of freedom in its purest state can be had watching these horsemen galloping across the immense plain.

EN ROUTE FROM AVEIRO TO ÓBIDOS

The free spirit of the people of Aveiro in the north is once again distinct from other areas. It was the boundless dreams of sailors that created the town's wealth, with its canals, tile-decorated houses, and stirring convent of the Infanta Joana. This is an active town, which has impressive rows of cod-drying sheds standing at the edge of the *ria,* bearing witness to an ancient tradition.

A delight that lies hidden near Aveiro is the little village of Costa Nova, situated between the sea and the lagoon. For more than a hundred years it has been a fishing village and seaside resort, and has managed to keep a unified appearance. The fishermen's houses, the *palheiros,* are made of broad planks of wood that are painted in white and colored vertical stripes. It is said that

TANQUE LAVA-ROUPA
UNIVERSAL Nº2
RIO TINTO—PORTO

It was in the nineteenth century that the bustling town of Aveiro had its façades covered with Brazilian-style azulejos (left). The vogue seduced all of Portugal, but it was especially popular among the "Brazilians"—emigrants who

returned home after having made their fortune abroad. They represented a very particular society, as depicted so wonderfully by Camilo Castelo Branco in his 1882 novel *A Brasileira de Prazins.*

In the Aveiro train station typical characters welcome the traveler: a fisherman, a fishwife, and even this "pretty girl," the *Tricana.* The panels date from 1916 (above).

each man could thus identify his home through the foggy *ria.* With a similar enthusiasm, newer buildings are also striped, but now the vertical lines are formed by patterns in the tile façades. Thanks should be given for this exceptional success to Mr. Galante, an engineer and former mayor of Ilhavo, the administrative center for the village of Costa Nova. The town's promenade, with its palm trees bordering the *ria,* is reminiscent of a painting by Le Douanier Rousseau.

A stop in one of the excellent small restaurants of Costa Nova is highly recommended. Try one of many recipes for eels that are fished in the *ria*—either marinated (*de escabeche*) or as a fish stew (*caldeirada*). Freshly caught fish from the sea also arrive every day at the port of Aveiro. The menu offers various wonders including *pregado* (turbot), *robalo* (bass), and *tambouril* (angler-fish). For a coffee break it is hard to resist creamy delicacies known as *ovos moles* of Aveiro, which were originally produced in a local monastery and now have a far-reaching reputation. Made of egg yolks and sugar syrup the candies are sold in small drums, or in the form of marine shapes molded in unleavened bread.

Further to the south, and inland, lies Coimbra, a town laden with symbols and washed by the river Mondego. Its university, one of the

It is a pleasure to stroll in the streets of Aveiro, where the elegant architecture and azulejo "picture gallery" accompany the walker with each step (top, middle, and bottom).

The university town of Coimbra is celebrated for its gardens. In the eighteenth century, under the reign of Dom João V, the Santa Cruz park was transformed according to the canons of baroque landscaping. Ornamental pools and fountains made their appearance. The Cascata, a high granite waterfall surrounded by azulejo medallions, is a highly symbolic work. It brings together the power of rugged, gray granite from the north with the delicacy of light, smooth, colorful azulejos from the south. This blue-toned medallion represents a biblical scene: the prophet Elijah throwing salt into the waters of Jericho. He is accompanied by the Evangelists, Saint Mark with his lion and Saint Matthew with an angel (left).

Portugal is the land of *claras-boias*, lanterns that achieve a delicate marriage between glass and metal, images of industrial progress (above right).

oldest in Europe, was for six hundred years—until 1911—the only one in the country. It was the incredible crucible within which was slowly forged a unified Portugal—now the oldest nation-state in Europe within its original frontiers. Coimbra, at the heart of Portugal, is a seductive town, where even the language that people speak is particularly pure and melodic.

During its long history, the city has adorned itself with all kinds of splendid monuments best discovered by browsing through the picturesque maze of small streets tumbling down the hillside. The university and its library, an acropolis standing over the Mondego, is the most prestigious example. Here even the inspiration of the gardens is intellectual. In the Manga garden, nature virtually disappears, to be replaced by architectural conceits. As for the botanical gardens, these were set up as a center for scientific research by the marquis of Pombal, senior minister under the enlightened despot Dom José. It is enchanting to walk in the vast terraced spaces, designed with

A moment of relaxation on the fertile plains of the Ribatejo. Here choice melons are grown and in the summer are sometimes sold under large tents by the road (top).

A typically Portuguese snapshot of the Coimbra market: a slicer cuts into thin strips the cabbage destined for *caldo verde,* the popular rustic soup (middle).

The Coimbra fish market is extremely well stocked, since fish is a major element of the local diet. On the ice of the fishmongers' stalls are found salted cod, sardines that shine like quicksilver, *pescadas,* gray hake with its light, mild meat, as well as the curious-looking *peixes-espada,* the aptly named swordfish (bottom).

baroque splendor and filled with plants from around the world, a fresh illustration of the universalism of the Portuguese, who are indefatigable travelers. The park created for the monks of Santa Cruz is another testimony to high culture. Here an entirely baroque and rococo setting, with dancing waters and pavilions, marries perfectly with a luxurious plant life, including the famed alley vaulted by magnificent oleanders.

When night falls here on a summer evening, men can often be heard singing a serenade or ballad, the *fado* of Coimbra. The local *fado,* which has evolved over the centuries, is often sung in the open air. It has a rhythm that is brisker than that of Lisbon, and its ancient and wildly poetical texts are accompanied by the *guitarra* and the *viola,* a kind of mandolin.

In the morning there is quite another Coimbra to see at the lively, colorful market. Here the constantly repeated search for "daily bread" combines with the pleasure of meeting friends. Women, their baskets filled with foodstuffs, arrive early in the morning and crowd into the market hall to sell their goods. Among the fish, freshly arrived from the port of Figueira da Foz, the connoisseur will find sardines that are so appreciated by the Portuguese, as well as tasty swordfish. These *peixes-espada,* long and pointed like rapiers, have a soft, silvery, scaleless skin that shines with the brilliance of fine steel.

The vegetable market reveals other subtleties of everyday life in Portugal. Here every kind of olive can be found—small brown olives from the Algarve, black olives of Alentejo, lighter-colored ones, preserved in oil, coming from Beiras, as well as Elvas olives—large, green, and preserved in brine. Nearby you can nibble on traditional snacks, such as ubiquitous *pevides,* large pumpkin seeds cooked in salted water, and *tremoços,* lupine seeds that have been soaked in water. These make a much appreciated gift for a Portuguese friend far from his homeland.

Coimbra, a center of student life, is also known for its cafés and *tascas,* small inexpensive restaurants and taverns where meals are simple and entertaining and the prices are clearly marked. In addition to a variety of *rissoes* (crusty golden rissoles of cod, chicken, or prawns) there is the *prego* (literally the "nail"), a beef escallop within a bread roll, the *bifana,* in which pork replaces beef, or *pipis* (chicken giblets served hot) and *caracóis* (tiny snails). At the end of the meal, there may be a *pudim flan* (caramel custard), a *leite creme* (custard made with milk and eggs), or an *arroz doce* (rice pudding)—all veritable national institutions. These desserts, often served in small individual terra-cotta pots, are sometimes decorated with charming designs drawn in cinnamon.

The region has a long-standing tradition of quality handicrafts, exemplified by the pottery and ceramics industry that was introduced in Coimbra at the end of the seventeenth century. The town's highly characteristic ceramics embody a curious synthesis of academic art and a more rustic tradition. Here, on pieces with quite elaborate shapes, erudite motifs deriving from Oriental or Hispanic-Arab sources are applied, but always with a certain popular touch. A variety of animals gambol joyously in the midst of a vegetation that is framed by artful borders. On the white background, the subdued greens, yellow ochres, and slightly faded rusts—that are not at all popularly inspired—achieve an intrinsic harmony with shapes that suggest those of lavish silver items. Another artisanal activity, which may not last much longer, is to be found at Lorvão, to the north of Coimbra. Here craftspeople carve toothpicks and pen holders in willow or poplar, ephemeral objects that were originally designed to decorate sweetmeats produced by nuns of the abbey at Lorvão.

A never-ending pleasure can be had in discovering the metamorphoses of Portuguese azulejos along the route to the south. Caldas da Rainha, for example, is known for its tradition of glazed tiles and is now an important ceramic

This region is known for its arts and crafts, which can be admired at, among other places, the Torre de Anto in Coimbra. This old medieval tower, which was part of the city's ancient walls, has been transformed into an exhibition hall. The area's superb woven baskets are well represented (left and bottom).

The area's most famous creation is undoubtedly its faïence. It is produced by a very old technique invented in the Orient, sought for in vain over the centuries, only to be rediscovered in Renaissance Italy.

The clay items are soaked in a bath of tin salts which, after firing, will form the fine, smooth, white, opaque glaze. Here we see potters' workshops in Coimbra, where faïence sits awaiting decoration (top and middle).

When the king, Dom João V discovered the ochre walls of Óbidos, he believed he saw a golden belt. A first look at the city is still a dream experience. The visitor should take a stroll along the ramparts and look out across the housetops with their gently flowing lines. The roofs are covered with half-cylindrical Moorish tiles, which face alternately up and down, with the upper ones covering the joint. Weathered by rain, wind, and sun, each tile is different—almost as if it were living matter (top and far right).

Although the town was partly destroyed by the great 1755 earthquake, there are still many Manueline traces surviving. Windows, doors, and arches are tucked away in back alleys. It was only during the town's rebuilding that color was added to borders, cornices, and plinths. These wonderful blues, reds, and ochres transform every home into a castle (bottom left and right).

center. Its reputation, already long-standing, was enhanced at the end of the nineteenth century when the great artist Rafael Bordalo Pinheiro set up the well-known factory that now bears his name. Drawing his inspiration from ordinary everyday life as much as from nature, he created works that were highly original. In addition to the amazing dishes in forms of fruits and vegetables and the zoomorphic terrines that the company makes, the Caldas da Rainha workshops are continually producing new creations.

The name of Caldas da Rainha is forever associated with that of the beautiful neighboring town of Óbidos, which was the domain of the queens of Portugal. Óbidos has maintained an unbroken continuity through time that gives it a remarkable homogeneity. The town is like a mirage. Packed within the crenelated battlements, over the centuries the houses have come to appear like elements of some vast sculpture. The flowing lines of its roofs set off graceful façades that are picked out with sculpted motifs and edged with ultramarines, yellows, ochres, and carmine reds—all tirelessly repainted by the townspeople. The layers of coating with their crackled surfaces seem to vibrate in the light. Bougainvillaea, solanum, giant geraniums, and every lush flower imaginable seem to be climbing to attack the town's walls, arcades, and covered walkways.

Óbidos is a town of extraordinarily beautiful churches covered with azulejos and paintings, including those of the artist Josefa d'Óbidos, which are similar in style to those of the Spanish artist Zurbaran. Óbidos is also a town of small artisanal shops, and choirs that sing to the strains of a guitar as the sun goes down. Óbidos is a town of artists—Maria José Salavisa, a well-known interior decorator, the painter Filipe Rocha da Silva, the architects José Fernando Teixeira and Duarte Cabral de Melo, and many others, have chosen to live here, thereby helping to preserve the charm and originality of this city of queens. Even the friendly, stylish local bar, the Ibn Errik Rex, is an extraordinary place. Here you can taste the tongue-tingling *ginjinha* liqueur, which is made with locally-grown Morello cherries and presented in crystal carafes, the *linguiças assadas* (grilled sausages) and the famous *queijo da Ilha*—the only true Portuguese cheese made solely of cow's milk, which originally came from the island of St. George in the Azores.

IN THE KINGDOM OF THE HORSE

The Veiga Stud Farm and its Lusitanian Horses. Portugal has always been famous for its horses, which are a constant theme of azulejo panels. Those bred and raised in the Ribatejo are so well known that the region could actually be labeled "horse country." Here breeders raise the prestigious Lusitanian horses—lively, alert thoroughbreds reminiscent of those mounted by the kings of France. They are particularly suited for *haute école* and professionals come from around the world to purchase them.

The Veiga stud farm, located at the Quinta da Broa, in Azinhaga near Golegã, is one of the area's principal breeding establishments. Its present owner, Manuel Tavares Veiga, represents the fifth generation of breeders on this estate. A second family house in Golegã is also encircled by stables and storage sheds for the harnesses that are kept perfectly maintained for use in competitions.

When arriving at Quinta da Broa, it is immediately obvious that the impressive residence is constructed in the same spirit as the surrounding estate. The chapel, with its gilded woodwork and frescoes, gives a foretaste of the iconographic magnificence to be found in the manor house. The dining room presents guests with illustrations of life and landscapes of the Ribatejo. The hunting room offers depictions of the finest game in *trompe l'oeil,* while the elegant stuccoes, imitation marbles, and handsome azulejos found throughout the residence make it a splendid example of nineteenth-century architecture.

In the distance, horses gallop to the horizon, their manes flaring in the wind. Surrounding the house, the broad esplanade is lined with the stud farm's outbuildings, at the heart of which is a superb set of stables. The large riding ring, indispensable to such an estate, allows for regular exercise and training of the high-spirited Lusitanian horses. The natural abilities of these elegant,

"In its smooth, fertile plain, in the melody of its cattle bells and the harmony of its color, the Ribatejo is . . . a fiery, scarlet belt around Portugal's waist," wrote Miguel Torga. This is the realm of horses. Huge herds graze freely in the *lezirias,* the fertile plains that often flood over. Lusitanian horses are reared in this province. Already known to the Romans, they were much prized by Moorish caliphs, who gave them as presents that carried a special honor. Later, Lusitanians featured in all the main riding treatises, and particularly in that of Pluvinel, equerry to King Louis XIII of France. Hardy, responsive, and full of character, they are much sought after for riding, *haute école* and, of course, bullfighting. Here we see the estate of a leading breeder, José Lobo.

sure-stepping mounts, help to understand how the talent of the Portuguese *haute école* riders can so brilliantly flourish. These masters of equitation can be seen displaying the fine points of their techniques each month at the palace of Queluz, near Lisbon, during exhibition shows given by the Portuguese School of Equestrian Arts, under the direction of Guilherme Borba.

This tradition has been kept alive without becoming ossified due to the *touradas,* or bullfights, which in Portugal are conducted on horseback. Another difference that sets off Portuguese *touradas* from Spanish *corridas* is that—since the

The Quinta da Broa, at the heart of one of the largest horse-rearing estates in the Ribatejo (top).

The *campinos* are accustomed "to the summer heat waves, the mud of spring and autumn, even to ice, and the strong winds that sweep the plain of the Tagus," writes Christian de Caters, a connoisseur of Portugal. The *campinos* are free men, lively and energetic, and are at once riders, grooms, herdsman, and cattlemen. Here a *campino* wears the traditional costume—a red vest and *barrete,* the long woolen cap that falls over one ear (middle).

In their house at Golegã, the Veiga family have brought together an impressive collection of memorabilia, trophies, and engravings retracing the history of their stud farm (bottom).

Evening falls at the Veiga estate of Quinta da Broa. As the horses return, they pass in front of the chapel of which the bells can almost be heard ringing in the fading light (right).

These superb harnesses would have been created for the occasion of Queen Victoria's visit to Portugal. They belong to Manuel and Maria Zinha Campilho, who raise horses on their vast estate near Alpiarca (page 97, left).

Two talented riders, Madalena and Manuel Abecassis (bottom and page 97, right) prepare to go horseback riding at Quinta da Boa Vista. In addition to teamwork, they practice dressage in their brick-vaulted riding ring. These two disciplines take them to equestrian events both in Portugal and abroad.

The Portuguese have always adorned their kitchens with special care. That of Boa Vista is decorated in the same spirit. Game, vegetables, and cooking utensils are depicted on diagonally-placed blue and white tiles (top).

eighteenth century—the bulls are not killed, and their horns are sheathed in leather so as not to wound the horses. The most spectacular *touradas* take place at Vila Franca de Xira, and Santarem in the Ribatejo, as well as in Lisbon, at the *praça de touros* of Campo Pequeno. The beauty of these *touradas* derives from the complicity that exists between the *cavaleiro,* in eighteenth-century costume, and his horse, a splendid stallion reminiscent of those painted by Velázquez. The placing of the banderillos and the skillful movements of horse and rider make for an extraordinary display.

A House with a View of the Tagus. Many of the towns of the Ribatejo organize joyful village festivals, such as the Colete Encardano held in July at Vila Franca de Xira when *campinos* on horseback take to the streets among a throng of running bulls. But the most popular gathering in the region is probably the traditional Golegã fair, held in early November on Martinmas Day for more than three hundred years. Main events include jumping, auctions, dressage, teamwork, and parades. In addition there are stands for the region's major breeders, including among others the Infante da Câmara, Palha, Sommer d'Andrade, and Veiga establishments.

This meeting is a must for devotees of competition events such as Manuel and Madalena Abecassis. Their specialties are *haute école* and teamwork. At the aptly named Quinta da Boa Vista near Vale de Figueira, the couple has recently built a superb house overlooking the Tagus. The stables, outbuildings for storing harness equipment, and riding ring—all designed by António José Brito e Cunha—are particularly handsome. Unusually, all of the ceilings, including

those in the house, are brick-vaulted, built with craft skills inherited from Moorish tradition. Azulejos also make their appearance—in the kitchen, for example, the tiles reproduce amusing, realistic scenes from everyday life.

It is a privilege to be present in this inner sanctum for the preparation of Ribatejo specialties such as shad, a succulent fish from the Tagus, prepared with bread crumbs and known as *açorda de sável, Caldeiradas,* or fish stews, made with whatever fish is abundant that day, or *caldeiradas de bacalhau,* a stew made with cod. Also delicious are the traditional broad beans that are a feature of Portuguese cuisine, served with *chouriço ribatejano.* A fine red Periquita, the lively, fruity wine of the Ribatejo will be greatly appreciated, followed by a dessert of *pastéis de feijão,* the unusual Torres Vedras sweetmeats made from kidney beans.

Adolfo de Sommer and his wife Adelaide Falcão have breathed new life into this *quinta*, a former monastery and vast estate that once belonged to the Knights Templar. Here the chapel, the arcaded cloister, and the huge vaulted kitchen are ever-present reminders of a past communal life. The pantry is decorated in blue-and-white azulejos with small, geometric motifs (top).

The kitchen at Quinta da Cardiga houses one of the largest collections of copper cookware in Portugal. It also features a large stone-carved sink (bottom left and right).

A Stylish Manor House. The Quinta da Cardiga is located not far from Vale de Figueira. This well-known monastery, which originally belonged to the Knights Templar, and then to the Order of Christ, was eventually bought in 1898 by Luiz Adolfo de Sommer and his wife Adelaide Falcão, and since then has been kept in the family. The Sommers, known for their remarkable energy, transformed this huge estate into a model enterprise. The corn, and more particularly the wine, of this *quinta* still enjoy an excellent reputation.

At the same time, the monastery and the chapel, which were falling into disrepair, have been entirely restored. The vastness of the medieval cloister and the refectory bear witness to the size of the monastic community that once occupied this impressive building. Hanging on the walls of the immense refectory—now serving as the kitchen—is one of Portugal's most impressive copper cookware collections. This huge refectory would have been necessary in earlier times when the owners of the house led a lavish lifestyle and there were always a great number of guests at

Magnificent seventeenth-century azulejos retrieved from the ruins of monuments have been used to decorate the vast cloister (bottom).

The view from this residence, looking out over the Tagus, is especially lovely. It can be enjoyed from the bedroom, decorated in the medieval style with curtains and small wooden shutters. The beds are covered, Portuguese fashion, with handsome embossed cotton bedspreads and covers (top).

the sumptuous meals. It was a time of wealth, judging from the vast outbuildings that continue to house more than fifty horse-drawn vehicles, Portuguese, French, and English in origin.

The house also has a fine collection of Vista Alegre porcelain made by the prestigious firm founded in 1824 by José Ferreira Pinto Bastos. Over the years, Vista Alegre table services and sculptural pieces—modeled on Chinese and Sèvres production—came to take the place of imports from the Far East. This porcelain was innovative and of excellent quality, and gradually became one of the essential ingredients of gracious Portuguese living. Times have changed, and there is something melancholy about the elegant ballroom, where the only remaining dancers are nymphs in the paintings. Yet the large terrace, looking out from what was once a strategic site of the powerful Knights Templar, still offers one of the finest panoramas over the Ribatejo. From here, across the river and the wide plains through which it runs, the castle of Almourol can be

The terrace is an earthly paradise confirming that medieval monks had a gift for choosing the most beautiful sites. Here stone balls fit harmoniously with the curved patterns of rocaille azulejos (middle).

A sumptuous life was led at the Sommer residence in the early part of this century that was so full of promise. Several dozen people were full-time residents of the palace, where princes and nobility rubbed shoulders. Parties followed one after the other in the grand ballroom, with couples waltzing beneath crystal chandeliers, next to allegorical murals painted by a French artist. Today the orchestra has stopped, and the house is filled with sweet melancholy. Even the marble statue seems to be dreaming of splendors past (top right). The piano is covered with a *colcha,* famous silk spreads embroidered with motifs drawn from Indian textiles (left). While the most famous *colchas* were made in Castelo Branco in the province of Beira Baixa, they were also embroidered in other regions of Portugal.

In most Portuguese houses a polychrome statue of a silver-crowned Virgin Mary will be found. Often they are displayed in *oratórios,* small, carved wooden shrines, which also display statues of the patron saints of family members (bottom).

DONA JOANNA DE SANTA IZABEL SENDO REFE
FEITORA ACABOU ESTA OBRA ANNO 1659

Thanks to the efforts of the Amaral Netos, the former monastery of Santo António has become a delightful home where the good life abounds. The former refectory has been transformed into a comfortable living room, elegantly furnished with English medallion-decorated fabrics from Colefax and Fowler (left).

The house is adorned with religious pictures, treated in the spirit of small reliquaries (bottom).

Dinner is served beneath the vaulted ceiling of the chapter house, which opens onto the cloister (top right).

seen in the distance, standing majestically on an island in the middle of the Tagus.

A Peaceful Home in the Franciscan Tradition. A number of monasteries in Portugal were turned into private residences after 1834, the year of the dissolution of religious orders throughout the country. In the 1970s Carlos and Maria Raquel Amaral Neto discovered this wonderful little monastery—the Santo António *conventinho*—at Pinheiro Grande near Golegã, and decided to rescue it from the disrepair into which it had fallen. You cannot help but appreciate the Franciscan sobriety and harmony of this sixteenth-century monastery, now meticulously restored. The chapter house, where meals are served when the weather is fine, opens onto the coolness of an arcaded cloister. Here, in the midst of scented flowers, a fountain seems to murmur stories from the past. Nearly every part of the building has been restored to its original function. The monk's cells are used as bedrooms and the refectory is now a large living room, a most convivial place, with an expansive white-washed, brick-vaulted ceiling.

An added delight is the disposition of the building. In the monastic tradition, the *conventinho* enjoys a magnificent view over the left bank of the Tagus. At the hours of vespers or compline, when the Franciscans once sang the praises of God's works, the river's waters are ablaze with reflections of the setting sun.

A HANDSOME RESIDENCE IN THE PORTUGUESE STYLE. If the memory of only one of these extraordinary houses could be kept alive, which would it be? That question could be asked with the appearance of each new marvel—including the Casa Anadia. It was built not far from the superb town of Viseu by the Pais do Amaral family, ancestors of the present owners, the counts of Mangualde.

There is a striking contrast between the sober façade and the magnificent interior staircase covered with azulejos created in Coimbra in the 1750s. As visitors climb to the upper floor, they are met by *Figures of Amazons,* inspired by illustrated Italian engravings. These large scenes fit within the Portuguese tradition of baroque settings, where the azulejos are not simply a decorative motif, but part of the architecture. The scrolled borders of the blue-toned tiling match the sculpted doorways.

The concern of creators the world over—whether artists or patrons—is to reconstruct space. But it is possible to accomplish other goals at the same time—to delight, to tell a story, to teach, even to surprise—within a highly developed conception of a certain art of living. Thus, in the reception salon, scenes from Ovid's *Metamorphoses* are lively conversation starters. A similar spirit seems to be sought in another room, where *The World Turned Upside Down* depicts, among other things, a father holding his child while the mother goes off to the war and a

The baroque staircase at Casa Anadia, the home of the counts of Mangualde, is one of the finest in Portugal. It is noteworthy both for its proportions and for its ornamentation—a painted ceiling and azulejos bearing the coat of arms of the Pais do Amaral family. In the baroque tradition staircases play an important social role, by welcoming guests and at the same time indicating the social standing of the master of the house (right).

The private apartments were laid out in the 1800s. The décor of these two rooms is reminiscent of the work of the great English architect John Soane. His neoclassical taste can be recognized in the small drawing room. In the bedroom, the canopy and lace bedspread are symptomatic of the refinement of this noble residence (top and middle).

It is easy to imagine the grandeur of the receptions held in the large salon, with its splendid azulejos. Striking cut-out borders frame and unify panels of various sizes. The soft reflections of azulejos in shades of blue and the passionate adventures of gods and goddesses inspired by Ovid's *Metamorphoses* create an atmosphere that is full of charm (right).

rider on horseback hunts underwater. Noble interiors with such an extraordinary sense of charm, well-being, and harmony are some of the greatest pleasures of surprising Portugal.

PLACES TO STAY

The road between Oporto and Lisbon offers so many discoveries. A stop-off at the wine-producing estate of Quinta da Sobreira at Vale de Figueira reveals yet another aspect of Portugal's wine culture. The *quinta* produces unpretentious table wines drawn from the barrel and served by the pitcher in local *tascas*.

The house, which stands in the middle of this prosperous estate, was built at the end of the last century. Its main salon was decorated by the grandmother of the present mistress of the house. An artist especially interested in painting, as were many society women of the period, she must have spent many pleasant hours surrounded by her family, designing the delicate flowery garlands that adorn the salon. A warm welcome is still assured by her granddaughter, Maria João Trigueiro de Martel Franco Frazão.

Countless unexpected discoveries can be made on a journey through Portugal. A visit to the Pousada do Castelo, which overlooks the enchanting market town of Óbidos, is one such gem. Encircled by the "golden belt of the walls," the castle was repeatedly coveted, threatened, and captured over the centuries until it was eventually reconquered. It is now a haven of peace.

Sitting in one of the very fine Gothic corners of the dining room, from one side the visitor looks out over the lovely flower-filled patio and from the other across the vast landscape of the Óbidos lagoon—filled in over the course of centuries—that stretches to the sea. The menu of this *pousada* offers various local specialties. Here you can try produce from the nearby ports, such as *sopa de congro* (conger eel soup) from Peniche,

or *caldeirada à moda da Nazaré* (fish stew that blends conger eel, skate, squid, eels, and sardines). The *bacalhau à Brás,* a recipe for cod with eggs and thinly sliced potatoes, is fabulous. To accompany these dishes, the wine waiter offers excellent local wines, such as a white wine from Gaeiras or an Oiro from Óbidos, straw-colored and slightly fruity. For dessert, local specialties include *cavacas* (crisp biscuits) of Caldas da Rainha, and *pão de ló,* a moist sponge cake sweets beautifully depicted in the still lives of the seventeenth-century artist Josefa d'Óbidos.

At Constância, the Quinta de Santa Bárbara has other pleasures in store for guests. This old house, so well located by the Tagus, once belonged to the Jesuit order. Since the sixteenth century it has been remodeled several times, and has always been restored with great care. Everything combines to plunge the traveler into the ambience of a traditional Portuguese home—salons with painted carved-wood ceilings, Brazilian wood floors, welcoming bedrooms with

At Quinta da Sobreira, an enchanting guest house where a warm welcome is given by Maria João Trigueiro de Martel Franco Frazão, the perimeter wall is built with curved openings filled by luxuriant vegetation (top).

Within this nineteenth-century manor house, the living room bookshelf is framed by a light-hearted painted design (far left).

In the restaurant of the Óbidos Château—now a *pousada*—certain tables are placed in the two Manueline window corners, offering views of the interior patio. This space, with its trimmed trees, is reminiscent of a *hortus conclusus,* the closed garden of the Middle Ages, a distant remembrance of an earthly paradise (left).

At the Quinta de Santa Bárbara, a large traditional residence that is now a pleasant guest house, a light, rustic meal is served on a stone table in the shade (right).

1
2
3
4

At the start of this century, Portugal's spa resorts saw an influx of visitors coming to take the waters. Like a true pioneer, Alexandre de Almeida understood immediately the potential of this new fashion. Born at Luso, near Cúria, where the waters were the most sought-after in Portugal, he built the sumptuous Cúria Palace Hotel.

In 1926 the huge thirty-three-meter swimming pool was opened, the largest in Portugal. You can imagine the enjoyment of the "sporty" types of the period, the girls with their boyish haircuts and the brilliantined young men, diving into its azure waters. Today, near the hotel with its old-fashioned charm, the pure lines of the swimming pool are suggestive of some huge cruise liner that would have delighted the adventurer Blaise Cendrars.

brick-vaulted ceilings, and the chapel decorated in azulejos that recount the life of Saint Barbara.

The restaurant is located in a large, vaulted cellar. *Sopa de peixes* (fish soup) and *migas de porco ribatejanas* (pork in a bread sauce), two Ribatejan specialties, are particularly tasty, as is the dessert, *queijinhos-do-céu* of Santarem, small "cheeses from heaven," made with eggs and sugar—a must in this former religious house. This is also a good opportunity to taste the local red wine, a Cartaxo that is lively, fruity, and dark in color.

The Cúria Palace Hotel appears in the midst of vineyards. The grandiose establishment, inaugurated in 1926, was built by Alexandre de Almeida, a businessman and *bon vivant,* to cater to the rush of people who came to take the waters at the fashionable spa resort. Twenty kilometers from the sea, its swimming pool, surrounded by fine sand and built to resemble a ship, was then one of the largest in Europe. Today the establishment has not changed and the service has remained faithful to the great traditions of Portuguese hotel-keeping. The hall, the corridors, and the huge dining room bring to mind a giant cruise liner, slightly underpopulated, steaming towards the land of nostalgia.

In the evening one can savor a specialty of Beira Litoral, *leitão assado,* a suckling pig with golden, crackling skin. This is also the moment to try a fresh white *rabaçal* (goat's milk cheese) and the unusual *manjar-branco* (blancmange) of Coimbra, a delicious old Portuguese recipe, in which white meat from a chicken is prepared with rice and sugar. The excellent wines of the region provide a perfect accompaniment for these dishes. There are fruity, tannic Dão, or deep-colored Bairrada wines with a generous, aromatic bouquet, such as the remarkable Luís Pato 1985. Wine sets tongues talking, and before long travel stories are being exchanged, including impressions of the legendary Buçaco Palace Hotel that lies hidden in the midst of the forest.

Buçaco. This is a name guaranteed to spark nostalgia in anyone who has ever visited the hotel, as did Suzanne Chantal, a French novelist captivated by Portugal: "A green cathedral raises its high vaults. . . . Beneath this sumptuous canopy of foliage at first all that can be heard is the muffled sound of wheels on the granite of the road, and all that is felt is a deep sensation of plenitude and serenity. . . . Here the light filters through a web of thin foliage, falls like rain on ferns, flickers off Hortensias, and loses itself in the thick velvet of moss and the deep bronze of ornamental pools." The hotel is like some strange, outlandish apparition at the heart of the splendid forest.

The décor here is truly theatrical, with a forest of pinnacles, gargoyles, gables, and lacy stonework arising around the keep. Designed by the Italian Luigi Manini, a stage director of the Lisbon Opera, it was built as a homage to Portugal's greatness in

At the Buçaco Palace Hotel, a meal is something of a celebration. One of the grand classics of its menu is the regional dish *chanfana de cabra serrana,* stewed goat made with Buçaco red wine and simmered in the oven in a traditional *caçoila,* a black terra-cotta pot from Molelos (left).

The cellar of the Buçaco Palace is a wonder. It is only possible to taste this famous wine at Buçaco, or at other establishments belonging to the descendants of the creator of this dream hotel (middle).

Cooked in small earthenware pots, these *tijeladas,* thick caramel puddings, and *pastéis de nata,* custard tarts, are a very Portuguese form of dessert (bottom right).

the nationalistic spirit of the 1900s. The project had been proposed several years earlier by the artist king Dom Ferdinand of Saxe-Coburg-Gotha, builder of the fantastic Pena Palace at Sintra. Although his grandson, Dom Carlos, never visited Buçaco, Dom Manuel—the youngest son of Dom Carlos and the last king of Portugal—spent some time here before going into exile.

The inspired atmosphere continues in the wonderful arcaded gallery, a Manueline reproduction of the Hieronymite cloister at Belém. A forest of stone, it is vibrant in the light, as are the surrounding trees. The interior is regal: monumental state rooms, doors, windows, and arches have an astonishing wealth of ornament, with their Manueline maritime motifs and Renaissance foliage, mingling with leaves carved in stone. Climbing the vast staircase, treading the red

Homemade sausages are delivered in baskets to the famous Marquês de Marialva restaurant in Cantanhede (page 110, left). Savory *rojões à marquês de Marialva,* a pork specialty, simmers on the stove in a copper casserole (bottom left). Another delectation is *queijionhos de cabra frescos,* fresh goat's cheese seasoned with peppercorns made in tin molds (top).

carpet that cushions the wide steps bordered with bronze candelabra—here each guest walks into a fairy tale. At the top of the stairs stands a splendid landing with extravagant Lusitanian-Hindu furniture, exotic Manueline doorways, and large potted palms. But perhaps the greatest luxury of all awaits in the huge royal suite, with its gilded and pearl-gray furniture.

The tiled panels that Jorge Colaço created for this palace of nostalgia also seem to have been conceived with the idea of stopping time in a Portugal that was undergoing traumatic changes. The azulejos tell epic tales of the Age of Discoveries, introduce the poems of Camões, the most Portuguese of writers, and make clear that the country's victory at Buçaco was a terrible defeat for Napoleon's troops.

However, and this is perhaps the real secret of Buçaco, all its grandeur in no way overwhelms guests. They are given a wonderful Portuguese welcome by an attentive staff, under the long-standing management of José Rodrigues dos Santos. Mealtime is a magic moment. During the fine season, in the neo-Gothic décor of the rotunda, the *floreira*, "basket," opens its festooned arches onto the garden, and you feel like a participant at some wonderful feast. The orchestra's music is the rustle of a cool breeze, chirping birds, and a murmuring fountain, mingled with conversation and tinkling glasses.

In the evening, after dinner, guests sit outside in the arcaded gallery. Night falls on stone columns that seem to turn into trees in this forest exhaling the scents of the night. A blissful pause; an hour is spent motionless in deep wicker armchairs under the watchful eye of heroic characters that seem to be awakening on the azulejo panels. Time comes to a standstill. Light suffuses the vast salons, where a young stone *trouvère* welcomes his guests. To relax here and drink a steaming herbal tea served from a silver tray, or to savor a fine vintage port in a crystal glass is indeed a pleasure fit for a king.

The forest seems to have invaded the hallway of the Buçaco Palace Hotel. Gifted sculptors have created a wonderland of lichens, mosses, giant ferns, ornamental cabbages, and festoons of fruit in the interweaving lacework of stone and carved vaulting. The woodwork of the windows, the furniture, and the lamp stands suggest coiled trains of ivy. The gardens are fragrant, and the scent of honeysuckle, box, roses, and jasmine wafts under the hotel's wooden ceilings and Manueline vaulting.

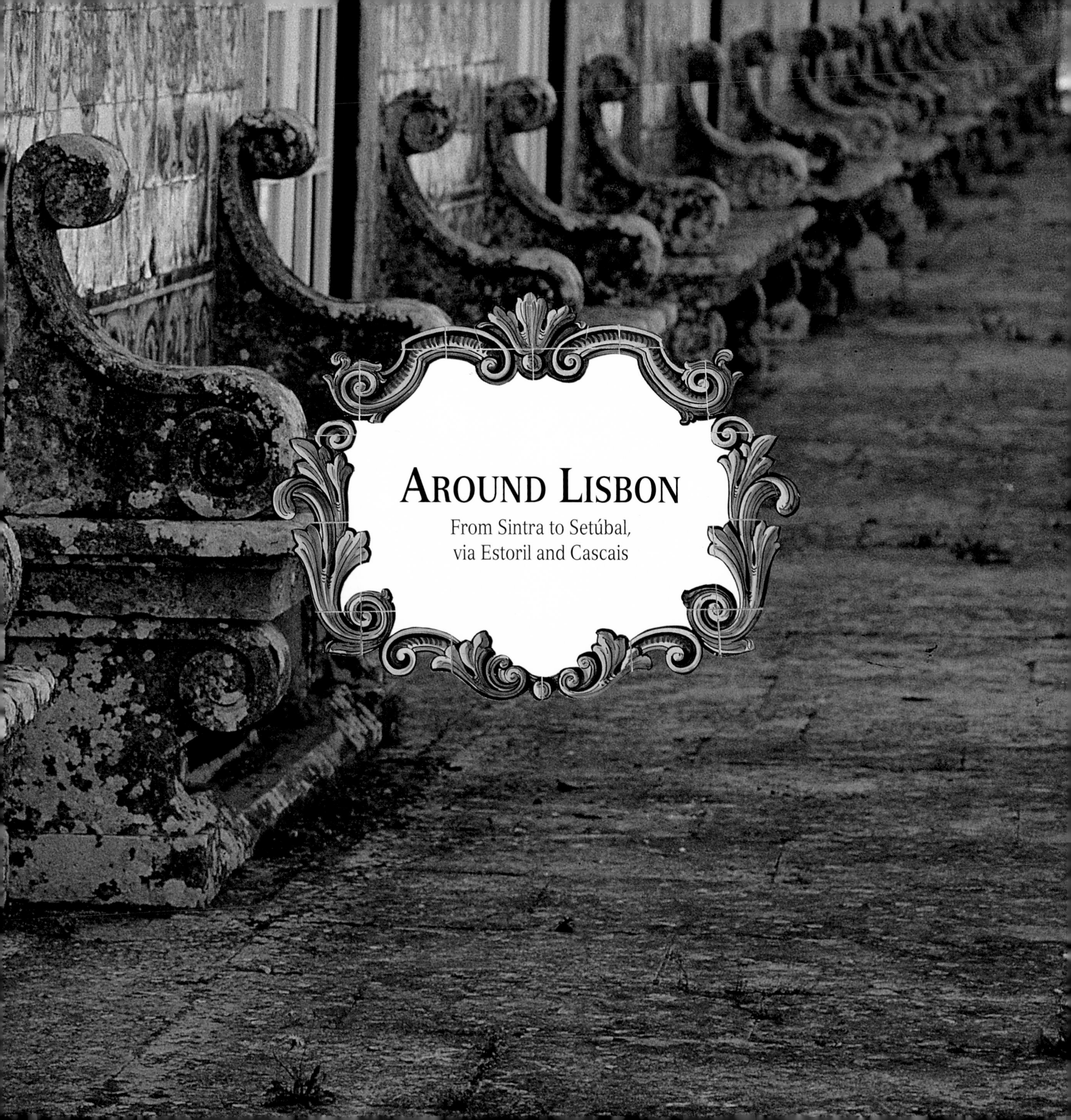

Around Lisbon

From Sintra to Setúbal,
via Estoril and Cascais

After the Ribatejo—the huge, seemingly limitless plain of the Tagus—the countryside around Lisbon offers a variety of contrasting landscapes, as if samples of each of Portugal's regions surrounded the capital. Off in the distance, the river loses itself in the Mar de Palha or "Sea of Straw," with its marshlands, creeks, and inlets. On the hilltops of Estremadura, the land of wind, ocean breezes turn the sails of windmills, producing a singing tone from the clay pots fixed to their tips. Near Torres Vedras and Mafra, the landscape is as most people imagine Portugal—lush, green, and rich with cornfields, orchards, and splendid vineyards. The residents of Lisbon love this generous land where olive trees cling to the hillsides, while on the horizon, the jagged outline of the Serra de Sintra appears with its lofty cliffs plunging through the mist into the Atlantic.

Anyone who has ever tried to plumb the secrets of the Portuguese soul has found it worthy of the greatest respect. Already at the time of the

A strange dialogue between weather and stone over more than three hundred years has left its mark on the Calhariz Palace near Sesimbra. These wonderful Portuguese benches between the French doors of the interlinking salons are inviting seats. Azulejos bear the familiar motif of *albarradas*, the flower-filled baskets that were fashionable in the 1730s (preceding double page).

At Sintra, a charming residence and its chapel are tucked away in the greenery (bottom left).

Rare and elegant dovecotes can be encountered by chance when visiting the region. This one is to be found at the Mitra Palace near Loures. The azulejos designed by Bartolomeu Antunes, with their polychrome medallions, blend pleasingly with the curved shape of the structure (above and right).

Muslim occupation, the Moors had a high opinion of Sintra, that "glorious Eden" whose praises were sung by Lord Byron in *Childe Harold's Pilgrimage*. The kings of Portugal followed the Moors' example, building palaces and taking the entire court to Sintra. The remarkable National Palace is a maze of rooms where even the floors are paved with azulejos and patios with murmuring fountains abound. And one wonders what dream must have inspired Dom Ferdinand of Saxe-Coburg-Gotha when this artist king had the fantastical Pena Palace built on the hilltop.

Nature is present everywhere in Sintra. The private gardens and the public parks of Pena and Monserrate, with their exuberant greenery, are all equally enchanting. When he had the Quinta de Monserrate landscaped in the last century, the eccentric Sir Francis Cook imported more than a thousand rare plants from all over the world, transporting them on greenhouse-ships complete with gardeners. Like so many others, the writer T'Serstevens was enthralled by these Sintra

At Sintra each house has its memories and its history. The splendid Quinta de Monserrate, which Lord Byron, William Beckford, and Sir Francis Cook imbued with a certain mythical quality, seems to grow like some exotic fruit in the midst of the forest (left). The Quinta da Regaleira also appears out of the greenery, with its lace-like stonework, benches, and fountains (top right).

Sintra, a place of a thousand adventures, the incarnation of romantic dreams over the centuries; Sintra, its praises are sung as if it were a paradise. On the foothills of the *serra*, which provide a handsome backdrop vibrant with light and shade, stand a series of historical residences: Pena Palace, the Moorish Castle, Seteais, Penha Verde, Monserrate. These palaces and castles were long inhabited by Portugal's kings and illustrious figures who created the country's glory—

cosmopolitan merchants such as Sir Francis Cook, or powerful aristocratic families such as the Cadavals, the Castros, or the Marialvas (bottom).

Seen on the horizon, the Moorish Castle, built more than a thousand years ago, is a romantic match for the sumptuous Casa dos Penedos constructed in the 1920s by the prominent architect Raúl Lino. He succeeded in integrating this wildly eclectic fortress-villa into the town that he loved (right).

gardens "where valleys full of exotic plants flourish together with ferns and palms among the verdant English-style lawns." This marvelously romantic town, with its narrow cobblestone streets, climbs a hillside that provides a grandiose backdrop, vibrant with light and shade, and studded with historical residences, royal palaces, and stately homes. The azulejos which decorate their interiors, and often the gardens, are an integral part of the Portuguese landscape.

FASCINATING AZULEJOS

Azulejos, the quintessence of Portugal, have over the centuries become the country's major decorative feature. How did this come about? The tiles are most likely an inheritance from the Moors—like so many other traditions in this country where much of the south was under Moorish occupation from the eighth through the thirteenth centuries. The term azulejo comes from *azul,* Arabic for lapis lazuli, a blue semiprecious stone of Mesopotamian origin. Azulejos also suggest an attraction for the Orient, which has always been strong in this nation that discovered new worlds, but remained distant from the main artistic centers of Europe. Another factor could be the availability of the materials needed for their manufacture—clay, tin, lead, cobalt, and manganese are easily found here.

Whatever their origin, Portugal's azulejos are a fascinating sight. It is a delight to discover them when strolling about—behind a high wall, in a secret garden, or in some stately mansion. Ceaselessly, over five centuries, they have acted as a mirror to an art of living, always closely in touch with the major artistic currents of the time. What is the secret of their beauty? Azulejos are more than narrative paintings on ceramics—they form an integral part of, and give shape to, a building's architecture, transforming the plainest home into a dream house.

From creators of illusions, the Portuguese have become masters in the difficult art of inventing a *joie de vivre.* At Loures, in the Correio-Mor Palace, azulejos are found integrated in surprising fashion with paintings and stucco work. The Gomes de Matta family—postmasters of the kingdom in the seventeenth and eighteenth centuries—were responsible for the construction of this princely residence, which is on a par with the châteaux of the duke of Choiseul or the princes of Thurn und Taxis, their counterparts in France and Germany. As was often the case, the commissions for azulejos were carried out over a long period. Serving as both ornamentation and memory, the tiled panels enable the visitor to relive the house's former days of splendor. Thus, in the chapel, the chaplain converses with a dwarf, two figures who, as William Beckford explained, were indispensable in any upper-class Portuguese home. The most amazing décor is that of the enormous kitchen. Here we find "hanging," in mouthwatering *trompe l'oeil,* fish, hams, and wild game.

A feast fit for a king in the kitchen and scenes of lordly life in a small drawing room—the design of the azulejos is always matched to the space they adorn. In the salons of the Calhariz Palace, built near Sesimbra at the end of the seventeenth century, azulejos blend elegantly with *objets d'art,* family portraits, and antique furniture. During the time of the palace's construction, the polychrome azulejos that had been in use since the Renaissance were going out of fashion. The new vogue for tiles in shades of blue, derived from Chinese porcelain and Dutch tilework, rapidly became the norm.

At Calhariz, which was built for lords of the realm, the azulejos depict various events from Portugal's history. Some of the panels showing victorious battles are even dated, which is unusual for azulejos. On these walls war is as peaceful as a dream. Clay, tin salts, and cobalt blue form an alliance with fire that gives birth to faïence—a

At the Quinta do Pombal the fresh air is enjoyed beneath a gracefully columned portico. Here, at the start of the century, a talented artist painted landscapes of Sintra in impressionist style. The skillful interplay of shade and light portrays nature with an intensity rarely found on azulejos (far left).

At the Correio-Mor Palace near Loures, the azulejos go together with paintings and stuccoes in a decorative ensemble of unusual scale (top).

A corner of paradise at the Quinta do Pombal: the *mina,* or spring, hidden in the mountainside (middle).

The architect Raúl Lino loved living at Sintra, in the beautiful Casa do Cipreste that he built in the 1920s. Here azulejos prefiguring the creations of Art Deco lead us into a universe of astonishing simplicity (bottom).

thin, iridescent glaze in warm creamy white that sets off the striking shades of blue. The large Palmela family often gathers in this fine historical house. Countless celebrations must have taken place within the chapel, where the blues of the azulejos and the marble go so perfectly together.

These marvelous blues are to be found everywhere. At Quinta do Pombal in Sintra the tiles draw on biblical themes to adorn a small grotto carved into the mountainside. There is not a breath of wind here, only the whisper of a spring, recalling the living waters of Jacob's well, the flow of the Jordan, the water changed to wine at the Marriage at Cana. Framed by delicate, neo-Gothic arches, the silhouettes of Christ, the Woman of Samaria, and the Governor of the Feast stand out against the elaborate landscape which unfolds on blue and white panels.

At the Casa do Cipreste in Sintra the azulejos introduce a different world of astonishing simplicity. Early in the century, the architect Raúl Lino traveled throughout Portugal in order to study and identify the particularities of the *casa portuguesa.* He then invented a curiously eclectic style, a kind of modernism coupled with a very *fin de siècle* spirit of nationalism. The house that Raúl Lino built at Sintra reflects that spirit. His grandson, Diogo Lino Pimentel, who is himself an architect, showed us the house's interesting Art Deco azulejos, which are perhaps some of the finest in the region. Abandoning classical scenes, Raúl Lino reinvented the use of the square and the rectangle, while still remaining within the

A leading figure of the wine world, António Francisco Avillez collects antique azulejos which he displays in vaulted wine lodges. He has also contributed to the setting up of a workshop for producing tiles in the tradition of Portuguese designers (top).

In the chapel of the Calhariz Palace, owned by the duke of Palmela, the blues of the azulejos combine marvelously with those of the marble. Countless family events must have been celebrated in front of these scenes of the life of Saint Francis of Assisi (bottom).

The palace's entry hall is a summary of the splendors of the estate as a whole. A stucco relief portraying the huntress Diana, imposing stags' heads, *trompe l'oeil* landscapes, azulejos, Persian rugs, and precious furniture compose a lavish setting (right).

great decorative tradition of Portuguese tilework.

These azulejos have come down through the centuries without ever losing their soul. Today much effort is being put into perpetuating the tradition. Thus, António Francisco Avillez, a leading figure of the region, joined with a group of associates to establish the São Simão Arte manufacturing plant at Azeitão, near Setúbal. The factory now produces azulejos in the old style. Also prominent in the wine world, António Francisco Avillez adds character to huge vaulted wine lodges with four hundred arches by displaying his impressive azulejo collection. The series ranges from the first Hispano-Arabic azulejos through to contemporary creations. His name is also linked to the renowned Lancers Rosé.

Countless walls in Portugal are celebrations of azulejo artwork. In stately homes, the choice of themes is often a function of the space available and the arrangement of the walls. The Four Elements, for example, fit on four panels, while the Arts and Trades fit on seven, and the Muses

At the Quinta de Manique, the azulejos were created over the years in accordance with the tastes of the time, as can be seen in the interesting variety of motifs. First of all geometrical azulejos, in monochrome blue or polychrome, were used in the chapel, the kitchen, and certain salons. Later, large baroque framing devices and monumental panels appeared in the dining room and the garden. They blend well with the handsome eighteenth-century Portuguese furniture to create an elegant atmosphere (left and right).

Horses and hunting dogs could pause to quench their thirst at this poetic triple drinking trough upon arriving in the palace's courtyard. As is often the case, this playful fountain is surrounded by a profusion of greenery (bottom).

Opaline washstand fittings integrate perfectly with the cherubs, fantastical birds, fruit, masks, and scrolls framing a tranquil rural scene (right).

Molha-Pão is a very typically Portuguese house, with its early-eighteenth-century azulejos. In the large entry hall, between leather armchairs decorated with exotic motifs, a frock coat recalls the splendors of yesteryear (top left).

East India Company porcelain dinner services are the pride of every good Portuguese household. Here they are decorated in fine gold with the family coat of arms (middle).

The broad, deep loggias open onto the cool of the garden (bottom).

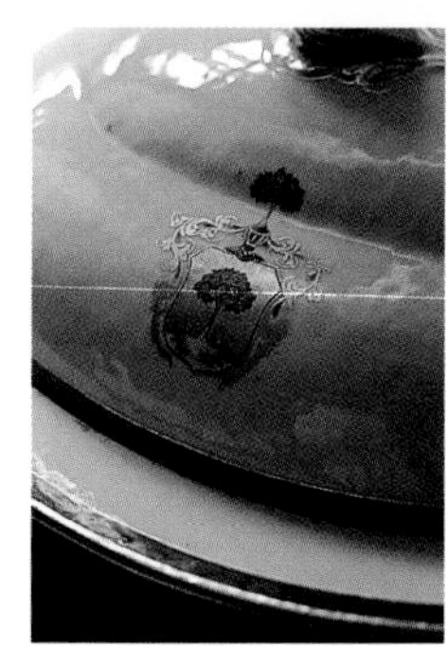

At the Quinta de Molha-Pão it would be wonderful to laze about on this marvelous four-poster bed of turned wood, an eighteenth-century piece much sought after in Portugal (top right).

on nine. With a consummate science of décor, these ceramic squares give added flair to the architecture. They contribute enormously to the charm of the Quinta de Manique at Alcabideche, one of the jewels of the Estoril region. In the salons, the tiled panels, which were created over a period of a hundred years, are a symphony of blue and white. The kitchen, one of the most refined in Portugal, is even more lavish than the chapel—an unusual reversal. As if to celebrate a ritual or a hymn to gastronomy, the arrangement of blue, gold, and white azulejos with their Oriental motifs is conceived with particular skill.

Outside the wind whispers in the foliage. The air is sweet and the sea is close in this lush countryside with its beautiful sights and fragrant scrub brush. It is here, not far from the capital, that residents of Lisbon choose to come, seeking the cooler climate of elegant *quintas.*

THE QUINTAS

The countryside surrounding Lisbon is populated with innumerable charming *quintas* or country houses. A *quinta*—a hard word to translate—is first and foremost an agricultural property, referring to the farmland and the orchards as well as living quarters with adjoining gardens. By extension, *quinta* sometimes simply refers to a villa—

a handsome summer house and its country park.

In the past, nobility, aristocrats, and other members of the upper class would come to these summer residences to escape the heat of the city and to oversee their estates, which are always well situated. Most *quintas* are found in places where water is abundant, the soil is fertile, or the land is suitable for vineyards. Others owe their location to the proximity of the royal palaces of Pena, Queluz, or Sintra.

Discovering these *quintas* is a never-ending source of pleasure. During the music festival, which is held in Sintra in the month of July, the palaces of Pena, Queluz, and Sintra open their doors to the public as night falls. The plasterwork of the ceilings, the azulejos, and the gold of the paneling seem almost brought to life by the music's magic.

At Sintra, other concerts offer a rare opportunity for the traveler to visit private *quintas.* Those of the Quinta da Piedade are particularly popular. This is the residence of the marchioness of Cadaval, a Venetian lady who has exercised her charm and talent over Portugal's musical life for more than fifty years. The musicians play in her gardens, in a symphony of blue conjured up by hortensias, agapanthus, and eighteenth-century azulejos that, appropriately, depict rustic fiddlers and country concerts. The splendid Quinta da Ribafria also holds concerts during the festival. As a guest for the evening, a visitor has the chance to experience at its fullest the *joie de vivre* of a Portuguese manor house. Mingling sumptuousness and simplicity, the residents of these homes have been able to maintain an air of poetic charm.

The Quinta de Molha-Pão. José Manuel Amaral Coelho, a businessman and art-lover, and his daughters, have the good fortune to live in a palace that resembles a jewel box adorned with azulejos. Their Quinta de Molha-Pão owes its name to the traditional "dipped bread" offered in soup kitchens for the poor. This strikingly

Portuguese manor is located near Belas, where the kings of Portugal maintained a summer residence.

Completed in the early eighteenth century, the vast estate has remained in the same family since its inception, keeping all the charm of a well-loved family home. The balance of the roofing and the proportions of its façade and interiors all contribute to the general sense of harmony. But the heart and soul of this quinta is its incomparable blue and white azulejo décor. They are found everywhere, on walls as well as on benches placed next to windows, where it is a pleasure to sit for awhile. The scenes of everyday life are depicted here with a thousand touching and picturesque details often tinged with humor. They provide a telling picture of the art of living as it was in Portugal early in the eighteenth century. Beneath garden foliage, a gentleman courts his beloved. Further along, a woman passes a love note during a romantic outing. Elsewhere, weary horses are shown drawing the carriage of a society lady, while another woman appears to be delousing a man fallen at her knees. Two wide arcaded loggias with a display of green plants provide an opportunity to enjoy the cool of the gardens.

Next to the house stands a chapel that is decorated with valuable eighteenth-century Dutch azulejos illustrating scenes from the life of Christ. At the end of the seventeenth century, the Dutch were the first to recognize the Portuguese passion for ceramics, and they began exporting tiles specially designed for the Portuguese market. Today the existence of these azulejos is a living testimony to the links that once existed between the maritime nations of Holland and Portugal.

The Delights of Illusion. Adorned by the celebrated frescoes that inspired the Sintra elite, the Quinta de São Sebastião is the entrance to another world, that of the nostalgic Romantic era. Looking at the delicately painted landscapes, which date from the early nineteenth century, viewers almost believe that they are seeing the distant silhouette of the *serra*. Before long neighboring *quintas* were following this manor's example, dissolving the walls of their houses to create an imaginary garden open to the surrounding nature.

The present owner, Helena Corrêa de Sá, receives friends in what is perhaps the most beautiful dining room in all Portugal. The walls are completely covered in frescoes painted in the style of the French artist Jean Pillement. Even the light muslin curtains are a *trompe l'oeil*. Frescoes also decorate other rooms, such as the Chinese boudoir, the hunting lodge, and the neo-Gothic salons that prefigure the mysterious dreams of the troubadour style. The historic relations between Portugal and England are again highlighted by the presence of Regency furniture, which has always been so sought by the Portuguese.

A Humanist's Retreat. Admirers of Sintra soon discover that it has an infinite variety of summer residences. The Quinta do Relógio is in Moorish style, while the incredible palace at

Built at the close of the eighteenth century, the Quinta de São Sebastião is a good example of the European aesthetic that was wavering between the established classical tradition and a new Gothic romanticism (middle).

In the garden, a charming pavilion is surrounded by blue agapanthus (bottom).

The landscape frescoes of the dining room are a daydreamer's delight (far left).

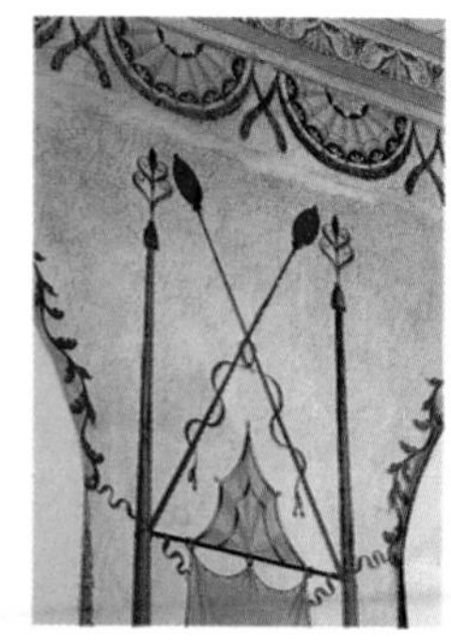

In the salons *trompe l'oeil* marble paneling in subdued tones of beige, yellow, blue, and red, depicts wall hangings suspended from slender columns and topped by decorative spears and a light curtain (top left and right).

The gardens adjoining the Bacalhoa Palace feature superbly trimmed hedges that are laid out to resemble an obstacle course. Further on the orangery, with its fragrant fruits, symbolizes the treasures of a paradise lost (middle and right).

Nearly five hundred years ago Dom Brás de Albuquerque, a humanist and a man of great culture, attempted to create a world in itself that might satisfy the needs of a Renaissance man—the Quinta da Bacalhoa. Today, it is still a pleasure to relax in the west loggia on a hot summer's day. Here the polychrome azulejos representing rivers such as the Nile, the Euphrates and the Danube, are inspired by Flemish engravings of the period (top).

The very Manueline towers of Bacalhoa, with their melon-shaped domes, (bottom) are reminiscent of those, such as the Belém Tower in Lisbon, built in the 1520s by Francisco de Arruda.

Monserrate—immortalized by Byron, William Beckford, and Sir Francis Cook—has an Indo-Persian influence. Each of these houses has its memories and a history all its own. Most of them are to be found around Sintra, but some families have always maintained their residences further south, on the Setúbal Peninsula, the Outra Banda.

Here the air is milder and the sea is never far away. The noble Quinta da Bacalhoa at Azeitão is famous for its Moroccan-style towers capped with melon-shaped ribbed domes, as well as for its azulejos and gardens. The present owners of the estate, Thomas W. Scoville and his wife, who split their time between the United States and Portugal, recount Bacalhoa's history. It was built during the Renaissance by Dom Brás de Albuquerque, son of a celebrated viceroy of the West Indies. Four centuries later, during the 1940s, it was sold to Orlena S. Scoville. She was passionately fond of her azulejos, which are among the oldest in Portugal, and devoted considerable energies to restoring them. Bacalhoa is a particularly good example of the ornamental power of ceramic tiles. Here they decorate loggias which open onto gardens in a Renaissance manner. The smell of orange blossom is all around. When it is hot, one sits here at a long stone table in a cool loggia decorated with polychrome panels representing some of the world's

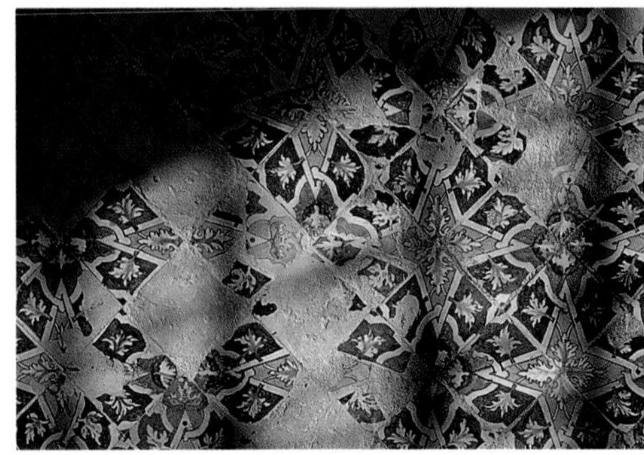

The Casa do Fresco stands in the midst of Bacalhoa's gardens. An arcaded loggia extends between three towers with pyramidal roofs, in keeping with the loggias of the palace. This very Renaissance style of pleasure pavilion soon became an essential component of Portuguese manor houses, with roots that can be traced back to the gardens of the Moors, with their irrigation pools and azulejos (far left and middle).

A highly sculptural series of interlinking doorways accentuates the effect of perspective. All the walls are covered with azulejos. Certain in the Mudéjar style, shiny and in relief, are among the last remaining from 1550s Portugal. Others, the *pisanos*, are completely smooth. The ridges that had been used to prevent colors from running into one another no longer were necessary, since tin salts fix the colors while still in the furnace (top right and bottom).

This delightful Renaissance-style medallion recalls the work of the French sculptors who worked in Portugal at the beginning of the sixteenth century (top left).

major rivers. A *lombo de porco assado* (a Portuguese recipe for loin of pork, marinated and then roasted) awaits, accompanied by a glass of the wonderful red wine of the Quinta de Bacalhoa. The wine, which has a blackcurrant flavor and is aged in oak vats, is a credit to the vineyards of the Setúbal Peninsula, suppliers of some of Portugal's best table wines.

A walk in the gardens reveals other surprises. Here everything is conceived with relaxation and the pleasures of the spirit in mind. Dom Brás de Albuquerque was a humanist. The Latin inscriptions and mythological scenes depicted on the azulejos of the garden's benches bear witness to his learning. The Casa do Fresco, a cool arcaded pavilion looking out over a large ornamental pool, is a particular delight. It would be tempting to take a swim here, under the eyes of *Susanna and the Elders*. This famous polychrome panel, dating from 1565, and in the style of Italian majolicas of the same period, is part of what has become a veritable azulejo museum.

Thomas W. Scoville is continuing the work begun by his grandmother. He and his wife are now bringing Bacalhoa back to life. In their desire to share the pleasure and refinement of the art of living in a *quinta* they have made the premises available for hire. The gardens with their many surprises are also open to the public.

These *quintas* are worth visiting for their madly poetic gardens alone. At Sintra each owner regards his trees with a respect that is almost religious. Those of the Quinta da Regaleira

The Quinta de Manique has always been a manor house with a tradition of hospitality. Not to be forgotten are the magnificent parties that were given here in the 1950s, when the marquis and marchioness of Casteja received the high society of Estoril. Here the exiled royalty of France, Italy, Spain, and Rumania could be found along with famous artists and writers. In those days Lisbon was a cultural metropolis, the kind of society that Paul Morand loved to portray. Next to the topiary garden, the romantic park lined with agapanthus recalls landscapes in the style of Hubert Robert—shady walkways lined with wide porticoes and a monumental fountain with all the majesty of an Italian palace (top and far right).

A typical image of Portuguese hospitality: these stone benches, decorated with superb azulejos, invite the visitor's admiring gaze at the entrance to the palace (bottom).

are particularly striking. In the park, among moss-covered trees and enormous ferns, all kinds of marvels can be found—a miniature cathedral, benches that are as solemn as mausoleums, strange animals, staircases, and mysterious grottoes with babbling springs.

A Manor House with a long history. Gardens are also a key feature of the Quinta de Manique at Alcabideche, between Sintra and Estoril. The present owners of the estate, the marquis and marchioness of Casteja, lead us round the wide avenues with French-style topiary. The visit continues in the park which, with its shady agapanthus-lined paths and wide porticoes, recalls the landscapes of the French painter Hubert Robert. The *tanque,* a large pool in front of the house, glitters in the sun. This traditional water reservoir was usually built in a monumental style. Here the water plays in a fountain which has the majesty of an Italian palace and spills over into picturesque channels covered with slabs of stone that serve as inviting benches.

Tucked away in the greenery, the manor house does not immediately catch the eye. In the eighteenth century it became the hunting residence of the marquis of Minas. Under this important minister of the marquis of Pombal it soon became an indispensable stopping-off point when the king and his court were at large in this splendid hunting territory. At first sight what is most surprising about the building is its apparent simplicity. But while the façade—often the case in Portuguese constructions—is curiously unemphatic, the interior is truly splendid. Here one finds azulejo-covered salons and an amazing kitchen. Here, the basin of a superb marble fountain is shaped to resemble the back of a donkey bearing water. It is easy to imagine the kitchen staff working round the great marble table, cooking delicious recipes that have been handed down lovingly within the family—the *lulas à Mariana,* delicious stewed squid, or the *ensopado de borrego,* a savory lamb stew that is one of the specialties of Manique.

The baroque dining room is equally splendid, with its polygonally coffered ceiling formed by moldings of an amazing boldness. To accompany the West Indian hardwood furniture there are corner cabinets displaying East India Company porcelain and gleaming silverware, both of which are the pride of every stately Portuguese home. The pleasure of dining in the midst of such luxury can still be experienced today. Continuing the traditional hospitality of the marquis of Minas, the Casteja family now make the extraordinary setting of their house and gardens available for receptions.

The Palace and Gardens of the Marquis of Fronteira. On the outskirts of Lisbon, the Fronteira Palace and its gardens are an invitation to discover yet other marvels. If it is true that people's characters are reflected in their creations, then Dom João Mascarenhas, the first marquis of Fronteira, must have had a powerful personality indeed. At the end of the seventeenth

In a different spirit, the topiary gardens with their statues and ornamental pools recall the formal gardens and the splendors of seventeenth-century France (right).

A curious S-shaped basin with edges scrolled like silverware, in a secluded, almost secret spot seems to invite the visitor to rest awhile (bottom).

On the main terrace, the imaginative ceramics are conceived principally as a function of the architecture. The space is punctuated by niches where azulejos represent highly sculptural allegorical figures (far right).

At the Fronteira Palace, the ornamental pool in front of the Kings' Gallery is in the tradition of Moorish pools. Certain of the azulejo panels here are clearly inspired by Oriental motifs (top and middle).

century, he had built what is probably the most imposing of Portugal's stately homes.

A visit should begin by walking through the French-style gardens with their centuries-old box hedges. The most spectacular feature of these gardens is the Kings' Gallery and the ornamental pool in front of it. Here it seems that the "warlord" Dom João Mascarenhas sought to celebrate his country's regained independence by laying out a sort of azulejo pantheon to the glories of his nation.

Fourteen plumed war heroes galloping on horseback are the first to appear. These heroically life-size horsemen, rendered in tones of blue, are some of the finest figurative azulejos of the seventeenth century, recalling equestrian portraits of the Velázquez school. Higher up, within niches, stand busts of the fifteen kings of Portugal; the three Spanish "usurpers" having been excluded.

When the weather is hot it is a delight to enter the Casa de Fresco, the loveliest grotto in Portugal. This "nymphaeum," decorated with ceramics and mother of pearl, includes, as is often the case,

precious fragments of delicate Chinese porcelain, some of which date from the late Ming era.

While the façade of the palace is inspired by that of an Italian villa, the interior offers a fantastic collection of azulejos. Dom João Mascarenhas, a learned man, designed his schema of ornamentation in relation to each given space. The noblest of subjects sit side by side with more narrative themes, drawn from both local and foreign traditions, so that Portuguese iconography is accompanied by that taken from Flemish engravings, Spanish paintings, or Oriental porcelains.

The Battle Hall, where tiled panels portray

Portugal's glorious victories over the Spaniards, is the heart of the palace. Here a heroic Don John of Austria battles with the palace's creator, the first marquis of Fronteira. Almost adjoining is the main terrace, which dazzles with the richness of its ornamentation. Together with azulejos that reproduce ancient ornamental motifs, there are Renaissance rocaille elements as well as bas-relief fruits and flowers in the style of the Della Robbias. The whole terrace, which is a profusion of flowers, features a series of large niches decorated with azulejos representing various allegorical figures. In this superb environment, one can take afternoon tea from an East India Company porcelain tea service in the company of Dom Fernando Mascarenhas, the present marquis of Fronteira, and his wife. The couple has established a foundation to set off this jewel in the country's crown, which they have now opened to

From the Quinta da Capela, which has been in the Cadaval family for centuries, one discovers a superb view. Today the house welcomes paying guests, who enjoy a hospitality that is truly unforgettable (top and bottom).

"This whole Lisbon peninsula is dotted with quintas, the country houses of an eighteenth century that knew how to live. They are sometimes the size of a château, but are usually no more than comfortable summer houses, with simple lines and fresh colors," wrote T'Serstevens in his *Portuguese Itinerary* (top and bottom, the Quinta da Capela).

the public. Among many other activities, they are researching problems having to do with the conservation of antique azulejos.

FOR THE PASSING VISITOR

Some of the *quintas* which dot the countryside around Lisbon are now open to visitors. During a stay in one of these delightful residences, the privileged guest is initiated into the many aspects of the art of living in Portugal.

On the road to Colares near Sintra, the Quinta da Capela opens its doors to us. This house enjoys a splendid panorama across the domes of Monserrate, the crenelated walls of the Moorish Castle, and the towers of the Pena Palace. By observing the gently curving rooftops of the residence the regular visitor can imagine the splendors contained within. In the harmonious Quinta da Capela, bedrooms and living rooms alike are furnished with simplicity and elegance. The charm of the estate is enhanced by the chapel that, in 1721, was covered with azulejos attributed to António de Oliveira Bernardes, the greatest Portuguese painter of that period.

Perhaps the most personal welcome to be had in the area of Sintra is that offered at the Quinta de São Thiago on the road to Colares, by the dynamic Maria Teresa Braddell. She was one of the first estate owners to have opened her vast residence to the public. People still speak of the debutantes' balls held here, where one could meet the duke of Braganza, the pretender to the throne, along with exiled European royalty. It is easy to feel at home in this elegant, lively, sixteenth-century house, with its collection of *objets d'art,* period furniture, rare books, and small chapel. Maria Teresa

The ornamental pool, in which a small rotunda temple topped by a dome with scrolled contours acts as an extension to the house, is one of the pleasures in store for visitors who choose to stay at the Quinta des Torres (below).

Braddell welcomes her guests to table, and offers the kind of delicious meals that are traditionally prepared in the kitchens of the best Portuguese households. Here one can taste the delicious *lulas recheadas* (small squid stuffed with bacon fat and cooked in a sauce) and the excellent *pato com arroz à portuguesa* (duck cooked in a casserole and then placed on a bed of rice in the oven).

The other bank of the Tagus also has pleasant surprises in store, such as the Quinta das Torres, near Azeitão. Dr. Bento de Sousa, the father of the present owner, was a man ahead of his time. Many years ago he began to accept paying guests, according to a practice that was already customary among English country house owners. The *quinta* is extremely suitable for such a venture. In this fine Renaissance villa, the entire layout is conceived with a symmetry that was quite new at the time. A group of four buildings surround a patio, and a loggia allows guests to relax in the shade, breathing in the fragrance of orange trees. Inside the house, antique furniture gives a personal touch to each of the rooms, and offers that indefinable charm so characteristic of lived-in homes. The dining room, which faces out onto a mirror of water, is decorated with precious Italian majolicas and rare sixteenth-century polychrome azulejos depicting mythological and hunting scenes. To eat a meal in this atmospheric room is truly a pleasure. Here you can taste local traditional produce such as small ewes'-milk cheese from Azeitão. Small and round with a delicious soft crust and a

The harmony that reigns in this residence makes it a most agreeable hotel. In its symmetry and coherence the villa seems to embody the humanist thought of the Renaissance. The apartments looking out onto the courtyard recall the tradition of Moorish patios. What a pleasure it would be to move into one of the rooms opening onto the terrace and write a very long novel (top).

A particularly well-conceived aspect of the building is the long perspective from the south wing towards the dining room, across the courtyard with a fountain at its center. The whimsical portico is surmounted by monumental pyramids—forms that are the image of a very Renaissance art of living (bottom).

Seteais also enchants with its cool gardens and irregularly trimmed hedges which, in their tight formation, suggest a flock of sheep mysteriously metamorphosed into vegetal sculpture (right).

The noble Seteais Palace Hotel is a dream spot for a stay at Sintra. With its vast esplanade spreading before it, Seteais is one of the finer creations to be found in the museum of architecture that is Sintra. Originally the residence had only a single wing. It was the wealthy marquis of Marialva who, in 1802 after the visit of the Prince Regent, built a triumphal commemorative arch and symmetrical wing with a principally scenic role (top left).

Exquisite hours can be passed in this elegant hotel, renowned for its beauty. In the bar and dining room, frescoes cover the walls with delightful imaginary landscapes, chinoiserie, rococo designs, and garlands (top right and bottom).

smooth, slightly pungent interior, the cheese was saved from extinction by the efforts of António Francisco Avillez—mentioned above for his work in producing azulejos in the traditional manner. This cheese goes very well with one of the region's best red wines, the spicy, fruity Piriquita. Then it is strongly advised to try one of the desserts proposed in what is still the Portuguese housewife's bible, the *Culinária Portuguesa*, published in 1933 by the gastronomist António Maria de Oliveira Bello Olleboma. The exquisite desserts on offer, often called *pudims*, are generally Bavarian creams, thick custards, mousses, and floating islands, prepared by cooks who know how to get the best out of the whites and, especially, the yolks of eggs. According to custom, these Portuguese desserts are accompanied by a port wine that is a marvel when served in a Quinta das Torres crystal glass.

Certain enchanting residences have been transformed into hotels without losing anything of their former charm. One of the country's loveliest, the Seteais Palace Hotel in Sintra, dates from the eighteenth century. According to tradition the name Seteais refers to the seven "sighs" repeated by an echo here. The majestic façade, in the English neoclassical style, is matched by splendid interiors with fine frescoes, some inspired by designs of the French painter Jean Pillement. In the grand salon, the walls seem to almost entirely disappear. Mermaids and maritime deities frolic gracefully in the blue waters of infinite landscapes. With a similar freedom of spirit, wild grasses and

Staying in a *pousada* is the best way to see Portugal's finest beauty spots. At São Filipe, an ancient fortress with a view of mountains and sea, the beauty of the landscape makes the bedrooms even more enjoyable and the meals taken on a terrace with seagulls flying overhead even more delicious (top).

Admiring the small campanile of a chapel, opening a door to discover some of the finest azulejos in the world—these are the pleasures in store at *pousadas* like that of the sixteenth-century São Filipe in Setúbal (middle).

exotic plants and trees branch to the ceiling, where birds fly and swoop. Dinner is sometimes served in this room, where the serenity of the environment adds greatly to the flow of conversation, making the meal even more exquisite. The furniture, which is all in the Portuguese neoclassical style, contributes to the extraordinary elegance of the whole.

LIVING ON THE COAST

In the area around Lisbon the jade green waters of the sea await at the end of every path. Along the coast, on the right bank of the Tagus, lies a string of little fishing villages, with their characteristic white houses. At Colares, the vineyards—with their famous Ramisco vines—are planted in the sand dunes, sheltered from the Atlantic winds. They produce fragrant, fruity white wines and light, velvety red wines of international repute.

Cascais, which in former days was a royal vacation resort, still earns its living from the sea. On the sandy beach, fishermen haul up multicolored boats, repair their nets, and bring their catch ashore. Here the ocean almost seems to have invaded the land, judging from the large black and white wavy patterns of the paving stones. Nearby Estoril, a noted spa resort, was a gathering point for Europe's exiled royal families, political refugees, and even spies during World War II.

On the other bank of the Tagus, the Serra da Arrábida and the Setúbal Peninsula loom distantly in the mist. Another world is revealed, a world that is almost Mediterranean, with its fragrant scrub brush mingled among pines and cypresses. The vegetation, the panoramas, and the golden cliffs plunging into the ocean bordered by sea caves make this peninsula one of Portugal's natural wonders. Beaches here are a delight—at Portinho da Arrábida, for example, where the waters are warmer than on the west coast, or at Comporta further to the south, built on a vast expanse of golden sand at the ocean's edge. Of great beauty also are the artistically painted multicolored boats—poetic pirogues with eyes ringed in black—moored on the beach of Caparica. Here, the pleasures of a small seaside resort can be discovered in the private homes and *pousadas* that have all the inexpressible charm of vacation homes.

A PEACEFUL FORTRESS. The Pousada de São Filipe in Setúbal is the perfect example of an enchanting retreat. This one-time fortress, built in the sixteenth century by Philip II of Spain, enjoys a superb view over the wooded heights of the Serra da Arrábida, Setúbal's lively port, and the estuary of the river Sado with its golden sandy beaches. The walls and vaulted ceiling of the chapel are covered with blue-toned azulejo scenes of the life of São Filipe, created by Policarpo de Oliveira Bernardes, a major eighteenth-century artist. Dining on the expansive terrace of the *pousada* is a wonderful experience. Mullet cooked Setúbal-style, together with smoked swordfish, a specialty of the house, here have a taste all their own. This is also an ideal spot to try the Palmela of João Pires, a fresh white wine with a hint of peach, and of course a renowned Setúbal moscatel. It is served young—after six years of maturing, when it is fresh and apricot-colored—as a luncheon aperitif beneath umbrellas in the open air. The older vintages, at twenty to twenty-five years old, are savored after dinner in the cool of evening.

A 1900 MEDIEVAL-STYLE SEASIDE RESIDENCE AT ESTORIL. The Fort da Cruz, built in the 1900s, stands next to the beach at Estoril. At the end of the nineteenth century this coastline became what Sintra had previously been for the Romantics. Once it was linked by rail with Lisbon, Estoril enjoyed the same kind of growth as the aristocratic Cascais. The arrival of rich foreigners, attracted by the vaunted marvels of the local climate, translated into a proliferation of amazing houses including Swiss chalets, English cottages, Norman castles, Tartar minarets, and Moorish mosques. Some years later the architect Raúl Lino and his disciples added a series of large villas built in a style that was equally composite—that of the *Casa portuguesa*.

Another time, another fortress. At Estoril, the Fort da Cruz, an impressive Roman-Tuscan-style castle, illustrates the tremendous spirit of enterprise that was abroad at the end of the last century. A wide corner gallery, with semicircular arches supported on a colonnade, opens to the sea. Here one can take tea with the lady of the house and reminisce about the history of this pleasant family residence (top).

The furniture and painted wall hangings of the interior decoration are conceived in the medieval style (bottom).

Celebrated by poets of the period, the fort stands as a striking testimony to the extraordinary wealth that abounded at the end of the nineteenth century (top and bottom).

Maria Emília Barros Lamas, the present hospitable owner, explains that it was in this extraordinary climate that her ancestor commissioned the Fort da Cruz, an incredible fortress built in the Tuscan-Roman style. Here every detail is executed with the greatest care. Even the interior decoration seeks to recreate a medieval ambience. The medieval-style furniture is imported from England, and the walls are hung with tapestries evoking scenes of the Middle Ages. But there is nothing fixed or solemn here, because her main intention is to provide a pleasant living space. And to take afternoon tea with Maria Emília Barros Lamas, looking out to sea from the arcaded Romanesque-style gallery, is indeed an unforgettably enjoyable moment.

Houses on the Dunes. In 1950, several decades after the completion of the Fort da Cruz, the Espírito Santo brothers—Portuguese bankers, figures in the art world, and constant innovators—bought several properties to the south

Robinson Crusoe, Friday, Swiss Family Robinson—these photographs evoke the lost paradises of many an adventure story. An outside shower, a rustic bathroom—the sumptuous marble bathrooms of palaces are far away and forgotten (top left and right).

These houses belong to the Espírito Santo family, which has always been ahead of its time. Ricardo Espírito Santo Silva was a leading banker who traveled the world in the 1950s searching out the finest Portuguese furniture and *objets d'art*. Today, his granddaughters Vera and Marina, together with their husbands Manrico Iachia and Luis Aguiam, give their holidays an ecological dimension by staying at Comporta to the south of Setúbal in one of the wildest parts of the Upper Alentejo. Here the calm, shimmering waters of the Sado marshlands are bordered by verdant rice fields and salt pans glistening in the sun. The fishermen's huts are built with local materials (middle and bottom).

Looking like a raft afloat between terra firma and a surrounding sea of green, this "permanent" house joins the charming holiday hamlet (far right).

In designing their seaside cottage, Vera and Manrico Iachia decided to adopt an ecological approach. A local craftsman, José Espada, who still masters traditional construction skills, was engaged to construct it. He collected straw, thatch, and reeds, which he then dried and cut to the required lengths. In the same way that the dimension of Breton oaks used for roof beams dictated the size of manor houses, here the scale is dictated by much less imposing materials. This explains the small size of these houses, which are effectively huts. The straw walls are reinforced by a wooden framework. Wood and reeds are also used for the roof, to support the thatch (top left and right).

An interplay of light and shade at the Iachia residence (bottom right). It is a pleasure to spend an idle hour here, with the sun filtering into the house. A Brazilian-style hammock is a sweet temptation (bottom left).

A cheerful table awaits the latter-day Robinson family in their adorable dollhouse (right).

Vera and Manrico Iachia on vacation (far right).

of Lisbon. Here a narrow strip of peninsula separates the sea from the fresh water of the river Sado estuary and shelters the small fishing village of Comporta. This is a wild landscape, where sand, water, wind, marshlands, and rice fields combine to shape an area of great beauty.

Not far from the main family residence, Vera, one of the Espírito Santo granddaughters, and her husband Manrico Iachia have committed themselves to an ecological architecture. They have followed local tradition by building a fishermen's cottage with materials found on the spot. José Espada—an ageing local craftsman skilled in traditional building methods—gathered, cut, trimmed, dried, and put together all the materials himself. A wooden framework supports the straw walls and the thatched roof, and a sort of reed armature serves as a reinforcement. The

brightly painted interior is decorated with fabrics and objects brought back from the couple's travels in South America and the Philippines.

Next door, Vera's sister and brother-in-law, Marina and Luis Aguiam, have restored a local fishermen's hut. This little dollhouse was so small that they had to enlarge the doors and windows, and even raise the thatched roof. Whitewashed and picked out in bright colors, it has become a charming seaside residence, sitting between the dunes and the forest with a low wall protecting it from ocean winds. Since these cottages must be small for structural reasons, each of them has an adjoining little "twin" hut. Nearby another typical cottage completes this holiday hamlet.

LISBON

Lisbon, as seen from the Tagus. Clinging to the hillsides, palaces, houses, churches, and monasteries combine in a sculpture of extraordinary harmony. The image could be a summing-up of Portugal: a union between a geographical location and the people who live there; a tolerance between human beings and the land they inhabit (preceding double page).

"Ah the Great Quay of the Past, from which we set off in Nation
The Great Quay, eternal and divine!
From what port? Into what waters? And why am I dreaming like this?
A Grand Quay, like other quays, but unique and alone." Fernando Pessoa, *Ode Marítima* (left).

The Viúva Lamego azulejo factory in largo do Intendente Pina Manique has one of Lisbon's finest façades (top).

Sailors on an oil tanker, passengers aboard a Russian liner, French seamen standing at attention on a cruiser, vacationers on a yacht, students clinging to the mast of a Portuguese training ship, fishermen in their small crafts, travelers packed into ferryboats, and even motorists driving across the bridge at twenty miles an hour—for everyone, whether nostalgic or light-hearted, discovering Lisbon is always a dazzling moment, a heaven-sent experience.

When the tide is out and the "Sea of Straw," iridescent with blue and green, blazes in gold, this incredible city is bathed by the waters of the Tagus. A thousand undulating hills seem to have absorbed all of Lisbon's monuments. A fortified castle, a white cupola, a scattering of church steeples, and a tower are all that stand out.

By simply climbing to the heights this sense of wonderment can be prolonged from poetic *miradouros,* belvederes that look out over the urban landscape and the ever-present Tagus. Spectacular views are to be had from the largo da Senhora do Monte and from St. George's Castle. Here, in keeping with the nuances of the Portuguese spirit, marked reliefs and outcrops are not leveled or laid low in authoritarian fashion. Quite the opposite—the city's architecture hugs the hillside, molds itself to the slopes, slides into the ancient tributaries of the Tagus, and slips into the valleys, as if it had been decided to leave the topography of the area in its original state of grace. This intimate complicity with nature is one of the secrets of Lisbon's beauty. In the older quarters it seems as if the houses have not been built, but have actually grown out of the soil on which they stand.

Such is the case of Alfama, one of the wonders of Lisbon. The neighborhood, shaped by the very length of its history, clings to a hillside falling sharply towards the Tagus. In Alfama a desire to see everything, to take in everything, is overwhelming. The streets tumble down to the Tagus between outcropping walls, interconnecting roofs, and baroque church façades. It is a

How many travelers, poets, and directors have narrated, described, filmed, and dreamt of Alfama! The writer Pierre Kyria saw it as a "magical labyrinth, full of hidden corners, traversed by winding stairs, lined by dollhouses with façades decorated by drying laundry, a birdcage, pots of geraniums, or with tall walls where ivy creeps across azulejos that appear even more blue in the moonlight" (top, bottom left, and p.153 left). Early in the morning the fishwives set up their stalls in Alfama's narrow streets (p. 153 right).

Stairs with wide, often uneven, steps are found all over Lisbon. While slowly descending, you wonder if this was once a green valley, with a stream rushing down to the Tagus. Today the building façades reflect onto cobblestones that gleam in the sunlight (bottom right).

maze of sloping alleys, steep stairways, and small squares. Strung from the house fronts, drying laundry flaps in the sunlight. Birdcages, pots of geraniums, and gardens hung from the garrets are seen everywhere. A bougainvillaea or a jacaranda flares with color, while above doorways, poignant little azulejo *registros* depict the Virgin Mary and patron saints such as Saint Anthony or Saint Marçal. Sometimes in the midst of a labyrinth of houses a huge palace with a heraldic pediment appears. Certain belong to famous families such as those of Dom Marcus de Noronha and Pedro Azevedo Coutinho. Others have been transformed—the Museum of Decorative Arts, for example, was set up in a seventeenth-century palace by the Ricardo do Espírito Santo Silva Foundation. Here, a harmony has been created between a diversity of neighboring elements.

This working-class quarter throbs with life. Small workshops sheltering artisans are to be found everywhere. The rua de Saõ Pedro market comes to life early in the morning. Fragrant

pyramids of tomatoes, cabbages, onions, oranges, and lemons are laid out on the vendors' stalls, and soon the cries of the *varinas*, the fishwives, can be heard. Carrying heavy loads on their heads, they call out: *"Sardinhas vivinhas, sardinhas vivinhas!"* (fresh sardines!). At midday, sardines fished during the night are cooked on charcoal grills next to front doors. The odor, so characteristic of Lisbon, filters through the neighborhood.

During the festivities surrounding popular saints' days, the alleyways are hung with paper garlands and Chinese lanterns. Pots of basil—the sweethearts' plant—accompanied by a paper carnation and a poem, are sold everywhere. When night falls, the celebration begins in earnest. A feast of grilled sardines, washed down with white wine, is accompanied by singing and dancing that goes on until dawn.

Forget big-city asphalt—cobblestones cover the sidewalks of Lisbon. The marquis of Pombal systematized this technique during reconstruction following the 1755 earthquake. In the nineteenth century the use of cobblestones became routine in towns throughout Portugal and the tradition is still very much alive today. One should take a close look at the sidewalks of Lisbon; black basalt and white limestone are arranged in an infinite variety of geometric and figurative motifs (top and bottom).

Sheets flap in the breeze coming off the sea and dry in the least ray of sunshine. It takes considerable skill to master the clotheslines running on a pulley system between house fronts. Care must be taken not to let anything drop down to the ground, four floors below. Meanwhile one can chat with the neighbor across the way (right).

Alfama is also the traditional fado district. As Christian de Caters wrote, fado is a “profound expression of the popular soul of Lisbon, with its taste for romantic novels, its instinctive generosity, its quickness to empathize, its spirit that is so close to *Les Misérables* and the *Mystères de Paris,* its love of tears, and its compassion. Even when badly sung, fado plunges its listeners into a kind of emotive trance. Rough-edged poems, unpolished words, unrequited love, betrayal, forgetting . . . all the hardships of a life that is either modest or poor, dashed hopes . . . passions, threats, promises . . . to a monotonal music of which the brief phrasings, the undertow of the rhythm, and the vocal undulations that come from plainchant, flamenco, and Arabic music, produce a pulsating impression. These are mournful lullabies that stir the slow surges of the heart and of remembrance.”

Fado’s origins are still something of a mystery. It is thought to have come either from Africa or Brazil. In the opinion of some, this nostalgic singing style was perhaps created on ships, sung by sailors during their long months at sea. Traditionally the fado singer is accompanied by a metallic-sounding Portuguese *guitarra* playing the melodic line, as well as a Spanish *guitarra,* the viola, punctuating the song with its fiery accents.

The legendary Amália Rodrigues, the purest embodiment of fado, has made this style of singing famous, renewing the traditional repertoire by performing the works of Portugal’s greatest poets. When she sings Camões, the poignant beauty of her voice seems to carry the spirit of an entire people. Today, other major fado artists draw on the poetry of Fernando Pessoa.

Each quarter of Lisbon reveals a new aspect of the city. The bustling Baixa, the lower town, is a quite different world than Alfama. When approached from the Tagus to the south, where the river flows by the impressive praça do Comércio, one has a powerful sense of the extraordinary bond that ties Lisbon to the ocean and to the

DORMIDAS
DORM

A wealth of Portuguese literature has recounted the joys and sorrows of everyday comings and goings on Lisbon's streets.

There is a hierarchy to the forms of urban transport used in the old city, based quite simply on the steepness of the terrain. As early as 1884, due to particularly steep gradients, funicular railways were installed to mount the city streets. In 1902, faced with a particularly abrupt slope, the superbly Gothic elevator that links the lower and upper parts of town was built. But the most common transport consists of the famous *electricos,* the yellow streetcars that patiently climb and thread their way through even the most difficult rush-hour traffic.

world beyond. Here, everyone knows of the drama that shook the morning of 1 November 1755: "They felt the earth tremble beneath them. The sea boiled up in the harbour and broke the ships which lay at anchor. Whirlwinds of flame and ashes covered the streets and squares. Houses came crashing down. . . . Thirty-thousand men, women and children were crushed to death under the ruins. . . . 'The Day of Judgement has come'," recounted Voltaire's Candide. The terrible catastrophe of this earthquake also inspired the French philosopher in his famous "Poem on the Disaster at Lisbon," and had a profound effect on Kant.

The city was never the same after the earthquake that would forever mark the collective memory. It was a providential opportunity for the marquis of Pombal, minister to Dom José, to undertake the reconstruction of the whole lower part of the city, assisted by the military architect Manuel da Maia. The originality of this project lay in the grid of streets crisscrossing at right angles. The extremely functional houses were in part prefabricated, the wooden framework having been partially assembled in Brazil. While all are similar in appearance, the houses are not at all monotonous, due to color washes of pink, yellow, and white. A sense of movement is given by the positioning of windows, the interplay of cornices, and the ironwork of the balconies. Even the ground seems to come alive, with its mosaics of basalt and limestone—the fascinating *calçada portuguesa* paving polished by the comings and goings of passers-by.

Much of the charm of this quarter at the heart of Lisbon comes from its bustling air of activity. Streets bear the names of various guilds and trades, and even today the rua do Ouro houses a number of goldsmiths. A door opens; one walks through to discover stairways and offices decorated with refreshing azulejos that were also created at the instigation of the marquis of Pombal. Ingeniously, these tiles have a limited number of motifs, painted in different colors and arranged in varying patterns, thus making it possible to combine variety with economy. Even during the urgency of reconstruction, the Portuguese never forgot Voltaire's adage: "Superfluity is a very necessary thing."

Baixa's streets converge towards the vast, lively square of the Rossio, where office workers, strollers, tourists, and casual passers-by go about their business or wander at leisure. In winter, chestnut sellers fan their charcoal embers and call their wares: *"Quentes e boas"* (hot and good). At the center of the square, surrounding two abundantly splashing fountains, a flower market offers a haven of tranquillity. Everyday life in Lisbon is made up of contrasts. A businessman buys flowers from a Cape Verdian street vendor, who balances the basket on her head. Cultures, origins, and social classes all intermix with a characteristically Portuguese fluency. The rapid tempo of a large modern metropolis is underpinned by the tranquil rhythms of certain neighborhoods that seem like villages in themselves.

João F. de Oliveira
MÉDICO
MARY QUANT
COSMETICS
PERFUMARIA
ELITE
CM
DE MACAU

Descending into the nearby metro station at praça dos Restauradores is the start of another enchanting journey, thanks to azulejos created by major contemporary artists. The train brakes at Cidade Universitária before Vieira da Silva's *The Metro* and silhouettes of famous philosophers. Underground at Alto dos Moinhos there is a charming view of Lisbon by Manuel Cargaleiro—a mirage. A moment later the timeless silhouette of Fernando Pessoa, as sketched by Júlio Pomar, flashes by at the Colégio Militar station.

With its many different facets, Lisbon is a city that has always held a fascination for writers and artists from around the world. Unforgettable creations include the *Requiem* of António Tabucchi, a melancholic homage to his "master" Fernando Pessoa; *Memorial do Convento* by José Saramago; and the extraordinary interior landscapes of the painter Maria Helena Vieira da Silva; Alain Tanner's superb film *In the White City*; and Wim Wenders' Lisbon, embodying the memory of a civilization in *Until the End of the World.*

One can catch a train from the heights of the incredible neo-Manueline railway station at Rossio. Down below stands the celebrated Gothic-looking Santa Justa elevator built by a disciple of Gustave Eiffel. Further out, in the Campo Pequeno, sits a Moorish bullring—the most famous in Portugal. Surprises are constant; panoramic views appear one after the other. Lisbon, a city locked into its long history, has never allowed itself to be fixed or fossilized by the weight of its past. To discover the city means to stroll about, to follow one's fancy. Continually going up and down the stairways, the visitor moves from one century to another, often happy to do so, as if the climbing itself helps to get a better sense of the city.

When the slope proves too steep for walking, people jump on funicular railways, such as da Glória, da Lavra, or da Bica. If the incline is less fierce, streetcars called *electricos* bravely toil up and down. Streetcars were never abandoned in Lisbon as they were in other cities. Climbing the most abrupt hillsides, they skillfully thread their way through narrow streets, all but touching the shops. On such a convivial mode of transport, a journey becomes a pleasant adventure, a privileged moment of the everyday, where time takes on another meaning.

One reaches the heights of Chiado, a neighborhood with a turbulent history. As Suzanne Chantal writes, "for the futile or the essential, one went to Chiado. It was there that fashions were launched, where gossip raged, where plots were hatched and where reputations were made and unmade. There one could find the best cigars, the most expensive knickknacks and the latest books from Paris." The terrible fire of 1988 partially destroyed the area, which is now being reconstructed. The spectacular building site overseen by the architect Álvaro Siza Vieira recalls certain drawings of Piranesi and Vieira da Silva.

However, even before the fire Chiado was no longer the sole quarter to reign over the city. Nearby neighborhoods had been undergoing a long process of rehabilitation. Lapa, Madragoa,

The Casa dos Bicos or "House of Points" was built by Dom Brás de Albuquerque at the start of the sixteenth century. Son of a famous viceroy of the Indies, Dom Brás was a humanist and writer as well as being councillor to the king. He had traveled in Italy and was a major figure in Renaissance Portugal. The pointed stonework of this façade is inspired by the Casa dei Diamanti in Ferrara, Italy, and by the Los Picos house in Segovia, Spain. Here, on the bank of the Tagus, one can imagine galleons unloading all the treasures of the Indies—gold, spices, and silks—and trading ships from around the world anchored before the windows (far left).

Whether it is the sculpted stonework at the top of a doorway or a cupola framed by palm trees, Lisbon offers endless surprises (top and bottom).

Large figurative azulejo displays are less common. In Lisbon several feature the work of the most famous ceramic painter of the nineteenth century, Luís Ferreira das Tabuletas, including the façade of this palace at campo Santa Clara (left).

During the nineteenth century Lisbon underwent a process of continuous embellishment. In the spirit of Art Nouveau, the windows of the palace of the viscounts of Santarém at Lapa are copiously decorated with polychrome bas-relief ceramics made at Caldas da Rainha, near Óbidos (bottom).

Façades are covered with azulejos in the Brazilian fashion. These are usually tiles with small individual repeating motifs.

and Bairro Alto have thus become the quintessence of a certain Lisbon. Stretching across several hills, these districts are made for strolling. There are streets crossing at right angles, from which the view falls gently, cut across by arcades and softened by the rhythm of the terrain. As the slopes become steeper the surprises are even greater, and the Tagus—with its sparkling waters of sapphire, emerald, and topaz—is an ever-present leitmotif. A single glance takes in the uneven pattern of cobblestones, walls gilded with light, a white marble cupola, and a giant oil tanker looming on the horizon. Lisbon—with each gaze it begins again.

Amália Rodrigues receives her guests in a truly beautiful residence; Alberto and Helena Vaz da Silva, leading figures in the capital's cultural life, welcome their friends in their marvelous house adorned with azulejos. But even the most sumptuous palaces, like the splendid French embassy, sit side by side with more modest houses.

As the writer José Rebelo explains: "Here, in effect, with the exception of Baixa, it is ordinary people—although who knows for how long?—who occupy the historic centers. Most areas of the city are still inhabited by a multitude of small businesses, all kinds of artisanal workshops, and taverns. There are few squares or streets that are not a village unto themselves, a reminder of what urban social life might have been like before the two world wars." Once again a journey through the city is also a voyage through time.

Luís Ferreira das Tabuletas is a true illusionist. His themes are sometimes very traditional, almost academic, with allegorical figures and very carefully designed framing devices of garlands and medallions (top). Below we see one of the most celebrated façades in Lisbon on largo Bordalo Pinheiro.

Is Lisbon only a white city? No, it is a metropolis in gentle hues of pink, yellow, and green. Even the reds are tinged with softness. As in the north, azulejos began to appear on outside walls during the nineteenth century, covering even the oldest façades with a passion. Like talismans, these adornments are always magical.

The rigors of everyday life seem lightened by the artistic polychrome coloring of wonderful façades, not least those designed by the painter Luís Ferreira das Tabuletas, which include medallions at the Campo de Santa Clara, as well as chinoiserie and flowers at the Fabrique de Viúva Lamego. Perhaps the finest façade of all is the one on largo Rafael Bordalo Pinheiro in Bairro Alto, with its *trompe l'oeil* figures that integrate perfectly with the architecture. There are so many others that it is hard to mention them all, but they include the huge wall by João Abel Manta near the Amoreiras aqueduct, and *The Dance of Menez,* which has adorned the praça das Flores for only a short time.

There are also azulejos to be found in the city's gardens, for example at the heavenly Quinta dos Azulejos in the Paço do Lumiar neighborhood. There, as if by magic, the wild exuberance of ceramic azulejos seems even to outdo the vegetation. As Christian Auscher realized so well:

Luís Ferreira das Tabuletas, a magician with color as well as a skilled draftsman, also left his mark on the façade of the Viúva Lamego azulejo factory. These tiles, painted with extraordinary skill, lead us into a very poetic world (details, left and page 160).

“Lisbon is not a city of green spaces. It is a city of secret gardens. Small gardens betrayed by a bougainvillaea appearing over the top of a wall. A doorway opens onto a lemon tree, a vine arbor hangs above a wash house, or rows of moss-covered pots. Balcony gardens, gardens suspended between hills and walls, between roof and sky. Carnations, bright geraniums, fleshy plants with small, luminescent flowers. Gardens on window sills. . . . Palace gardens surrounded by high walls, that no one ever visits.”

In order to best enjoy Lisbon in all its variety some people prefer to take a certain distance. Such is the case of architect António Teixeira Guerra and his wife Martine. The fine residence, which they have built high up on the other shore of the Tagus, is conceived as a sort of jewel box, a belvedere taking in the wonderful panorama of the city from dawn till dusk.

Here, as if to soften the imperious power of perspectives and components, large white arcades frame the view on all sides and form a counterpoint to the elegant curves of the suspension bridge spanning the river. From Saint George’s Castle to the mouth of the Tagus, via the Belém Tower, each section of the city passes before one’s eyes.

To the west, on the bank of the Tagus, Belém, with its splendid Manueline monuments, monastery, cloister, and tower is an eloquent testimony to the driving spirit that once carried this nation to the ends of the earth. The new cultural center is yet another stage in this journey.

“Stained, broken, or cracked, azulejos remain the most beautiful flower of any enclosure; they bring life to the austerity of trimmed hedges, cause the green of lawns to sing, distribute their rare colors with a boldness that sometimes borders on licentiousness,” wrote Paul Morand. The garden of the Quinta dos Azulejos, whose praises have been sung by poets and chroniclers alike, is decorated with an incredible profusion of ceramics and azulejos. The main walkway seems to have been conceived in order to exploit all the decorative possibilities of polychrome azulejos. The backs of the benches are inspired by romantic and bucolic scenes in the style of Watteau (left).

Through the magic of faïence, an arch becomes a noble baroque portal (top).

A superb example of a rococo garden, where the azulejos, abandoning flat surfaces, are molded like sculptures (bottom).

In the old-fashioned surroundings of the Antiga Confeitaria in Belém, people carry out or enjoy at the counter the delicious custard tarts called *pastéis de Belém.* The scent of cinnamon, sprinkled on the pastries, hangs in the air (left). Customers also come to the famous Lisbon pastry shop to drink a *galão*, a large coffee with milk, served in a glass (right).

The Cervejaria Trindade has the warmth and ambience of a brasserie, and the beer is delicious. In this former refectory of the Trinidade monastery, the masonic symbols of the azulejos provide added interest for diners (bottom).

Pastéis are stacked face to face to keep the cream from cooling off. The cakes have been made since 1837, following a very old recipe from the monastery of the Hieronymites of Belém (above).

Palaces and picturesque houses sit side by side in Belém, all facing out towards the Tagus. Here, of course, as in all of Lisbon, people love to get together, chatting for hours on end.

A RENDEZVOUS IN LISBON

The people of Lisbon, always very sociable, like to meet over a cup of coffee, have a drink together, share the delights of Portuguese cuisine, or settle into a calm spot at the heart of the bustling city and discover Lisbon by night.

One favorite haunt is the Antiga Confeitaria in Belém, where customers come for the *pastéis de Belém,* cream tarts for which the recipe is still a jealously guarded secret. Tasting them at any hour of the day along with a small cup of coffee is always a moment worth savoring. In Portugal the coffee is delicious, since the country's former colonies including Brazil, Angola, Timor, and the Cape Verde Islands, are coffee-producing countries. A coffee can be ordered in any number of

Between two errands or appointments in Baixa, try to find this tiny tavern near the church of São Domingos. It is well worth the search to savor a *ginjinha,* the delicious Morello cherry liqueur that gives the bar its name (top).

At the renowned Versailles café-restaurant, the mirrors still reflect the golden age of Lisbon's grand cafés (bottom).

Typically Portuguese, life-size welcoming figures depicted on azulejos recall court life and its rules of etiquette. Invented in the eighteenth century, they accord with the baroque taste for surprise theatrical effects and *trompe l'oeil.* The tradition continues at the Antiga Confeitaria in Belém (right).

different ways—very light, it is a *carioca;* served in a cup with a little milk it is a *garoto;* a large milky coffee served in a glass is called a *galão;* and with a bit of brandy it is a lightly scented *bica com cheirinho.*

Here the drinking of a coffee—*uma bica*—is a veritable institution. Lisbon's cafés still play a very important social role, although they no longer have the aura of the days when the Café Nicola and the Chave d'Ouro were at their height. And while the pace of life has changed, a bronze Fernando Pessoa still keeps watch in front of the Brasileira Café in Chiado, where the poet was a frequent visitor.

Another popular beverage in Lisbon is *ginja* or *ginjinha,* a delightful liqueur made by macerating Morello cherries, *ginjas,* which grow so well in Estremadura. Although found all over the city, it is a particular pleasure to sip a small glass in the tiny haven of A Ginjinha, a much patronized tavern near the church of São Domingos on the Rossio.

At midday the city's bars and restaurants are packed. In the Baixa neighborhood, piles of *pastéis* (small pastries), *crepes* (thin pancakes), *croquetes* (croquettes), *chamussas* (pastry triangles) and *rissóis* (rissoles) filled with rice, meat, cod, or prawns are on offer, and are all faintly suggestive of Oriental cuisine. These various offerings, often served fried, and always well browned and crispy, provide a light and delicious meal. They are usually accompanied by a typical *salada mixta* (mixed salad) in which lettuce, pepper, sweet onion, and grated carrots combine to such good effect.

It might be a bit noisy, but another very popular meeting place is the famous Cervejaria Trindade, where students and journalists from Bairro Alto gather. The beer is delicious and the small garden is filled with the scent of jasmine. Inside, the main room is famous for its polychrome azulejos; panels representing allegorical figures and masonic emblems are the work of

Luís Ferreira das Tabuletas, a leading nineteenth-century azulejo artist.

In Chiado, members invite their friends to meet them at the fashionable Grémio Literario, the most celebrated private club in Lisbon. Founded in 1846 by leading liberal industrialists who wanted to bring together artists and intellectuals from all walks of life, the club has a tradition of being open to all political and cultural tendencies. Today it is honored to have as one of its more prestigious members the president of the Republic, Mário Soares.

Currently Geraldo Salles Lane presides over the Grémio Literario, which is located in a fine nineteenth-century building. The club's furniture and *objets d'art*—including works by Gallé and Mucha—create an elegant, subdued atmosphere. The heart of the building is the library, but the restaurant is also a key element.

The dining room overlooks one of those extraordinary Lisbon gardens where a relatively small space is turned into an enchanting domain. Eça de Queiroz, a great nineteenth-century Portuguese writer and member of the club, called it "my *quinta* in Chiado." There are creepers climbing up the high walls, captured greenery that falls with grace, fragrantly flowered trees, a refreshing fountain, and, far beyond this secret garden, the insistent presence of the Tagus as an opening to the outside world.

The Grémio Literario is renowned for its cuisine. Here one can taste a number of traditional recipes, including a Lisbon specialty with literary influences, the *ameijoas à Bulhão Pato,* a delicious dish of braised clams. The recipe was created in the 1800s by the writer Bulhão Pato, a member of the club and a lover of culinary art. One can also savor another creation, invented in the days of the marquis of Pombal: *bacalhau gratinado com natas,* a delicious cod dish served au gratin with fresh cream.

Although Chiado no longer reigns supreme over fashionable Lisbon, the Aviz restaurant—

For some years now an ambitious restoration project has been bringing back the charm of Bairro Alto. An interplay of lights glows on this historic neighborhood which, both night and day, is one of the most picturesque in Lisbon (left).

one of its finest jewels—should not be missed at dinner time. This famous establishment was set up almost thirty years ago by the staff of the Aviz Hotel (now gone), where the great patron of the arts, Calouste Gulbenkian, once lived. On arriving, the *trompe l'oeil* azulejos of welcoming figures give a foretaste of the delights to come.

In an elegant ambience beneath the golden chandeliers, the service is truly perfect. Specialties such as *robalo à portuguesa* (Portuguese-style bass served with tomatoes) or the *costeletas de porco recheadas com ameijoas* (pork chops stuffed with clams) give an opportunity to discover the finesse of Portuguese cuisine.

The fashion for rustic dishes could easily overshadow the existence of this more refined cuisine. Fortunately this is not the case. To be convinced one need only push open the door of the Casa da Comida. The bar, adorned with East India Company porcelain, and the dining room with its captivating palm tree offer a very pleasant environment where politicians and prominent Lisbon figures meet. Jorge Vale, who officiates here, offers among other marvels a *pregado com pimenta verde* (turbot with green pepper), and a great Estremadura classic, the excellent *faisão à moda do Convento de Alcântara,* pheasant marinated in port and stuffed

One of the most poetic bars in Lisbon is the Pavilhão Chinês, the "Chinese Pavilion." This is the place to come to take afternoon tea, or to drink excellent cocktails from dusk to dawn. The bar's extraordinary setting, with its subdued atmosphere, is described by the writer Jacques Damade in *Lisbonne, la nostalgie du futur:* "Within the display cases, by hundreds, gleaming like enameled azulejos, but deeply, in relief, lives a kitsch humanity that dates from about a half century ago. A thousand figurines . . . parade behind the glass . . . of tall cabinets that entirely cover the four sides of the café. . . . The objects are collected with such coherence, such a manic obsession, that it is dizzying, disturbing even" (top and bottom).

Lisbon high society meets at the Alcântara Café, designed by António Pinto. Contrasting with the restaurant—a hymn to the beauty of metal—the bar is more intimate, recalling the comfort of English pubs (bottom).

A fashionable night club not far from the Tagus dockside, the XXIV de Julho (24 July) is a highly successful design by the interior decorator Pedro Luz. Stars seem to shoot out from among tall columns and the three flights of the grand staircase. The city's gilded youth gathers in this luxurious environment, drawn by the quality of the music and the perfect cocktails (top left and far right).

with truffles. As a dessert, one has the option of another typically Portuguese dish, an authentically prepared egg *pudim.*

At nightfall the city assumes an air of gentle mystery. The Tagus seems to disappear into the distance, and the thousand and one hills beckon you to take a surprise-filled journey. Evenings often begin in the Bairro Alto that Manuel Reis—one of the kings of Lisbon's night life—popularized with his famous night club, the Frágil. You sometimes hear, at the turn of a corner, the mournful notes of a fado escaping through the half-open door of a *tasca.*

The magical Pavilhão Chinês bar has an entirely different atmosphere. The display cabinets lining the walls house a veritable inventory in the manner of Jacques Prévert: airplanes, lead soldiers, porcelain dancers, ceramics by Rafael Bordalo Pinheiro, and hundreds of other unwonted things. Once rescued from anonymity by Luís Pinto Coelho, each article seems to have taken on a life of its own.

Near the Tagus, in a fashionable neighborhood now undergoing major rehabilitation, another place and another time await. Ultramodern bars, designed by well-known interior decorators, line the quayside. The evening begins at a restaurant that plunges the night owl into an Art Deco Lisbon—the Alcântara Café, recently redesigned by the interior decorator António Pinto. The metallic architecture of this former warehouse—with an extraordinary décor of columns and pilasters, as well as an amazing bronze-colored Victory of Samothrace—accentuated by mirrors, creates a lively and unexpected atmosphere that makes it one of Lisbon's favorite nightspots. Later, friends are met at the XXIV de Julho, a night club where the cosmic decoration by Pedro Luz takes one on a voyage to the limits of the universe. Another famed discotheque, the Kapital, is a surrealist world invented by the interior architect Maria José Salavisa.

Lisbon, a metropolis so marked by other peoples and faraway places, is a city one is reluctant to leave. Whether to stay in its classic hotels, to venture to the heights of the vantage points that provide such splendid panoramas over the city, or explore the secrets hidden behind high walls in the older quarters—must one really choose? It might be enough to book a room at the York House Hotel. Located near the elegant Lapa neighborhood and the French embassy, the hotel is situated in a former seventeenth-century monastery. One quickly forgets the din of the city when climbing the steps hidden between two age-old walls. The patio is a cool oasis where birds sing. The salons, the bedrooms, the balance of the hotel's proportions, interior decoration and furniture—everything has the appeal of an old palace that never faded. Graham Greene, Teixeira de Pascoaes, Vieira da Silva and Marguerite Duras all fell under the hotel's charm. Furniture made of exotic woods, Arraiolos carpets, and azulejos enchant the passing visitor.

The Casa da Comida is the way one would like a restaurant to be—refined, simple, and supremely Portuguese. From the entrance, the bar, with its wood paneling and *objets d'art*, suggests an elegant private home. The tables are arranged around the sort of charming little garden so often found in Lisbon—with a fountain, abundant greenery, and roses. Here one can enjoy the cooking of Jorge Vale, prepared with the best produce, fresh from the market (top).

The Gremio Literario, in the historic neighborhood of Chiado, is Lisbon's most prestigious private club. Geraldo Salles Lane, an intellectual and expert in making daily life an art, is the current president of the club. Above right we see the doorman of this important center for Lisbon society.

Hidden behind high walls, the legendary York House is a retreat in the center of town. It could be a Lisbon palace as depicted by Eça de Queiroz, a manor house as described by Camilo Castelo Branco, or the sort of hotel that Paul Morand and Valéry Larbaud would have loved. Here one discovers an exotic Lisbon in the shade of the patio's palm tree, as well as a timeless Lisbon, with its four-poster beds under high wooden ceilings (bottom and right).

Nearby, in what was once part of the estate of the Discalced Friars, the Cerâmica Constância offers an opportunity to see how azulejos are made. In this famous establishment, set up over one hundred and fifty years ago, one marvels at the prodigious wealth of a decorative art that has been constantly enriched over the centuries—in terms of both iconography and techniques—with Hispano-Arabic, Italian, Far Eastern, Dutch, and French elements. The managing director, Dom Francisco de Almeida, shows us around his workshops where azulejos are made both in the old manner and by using new techniques such as silkscreen printing. Similarly, painters reproduce antique patterns, but they also create new works. One of their great successes is the monumental retaining wall of polychrome azulejos on Calouste Gulbenkian Avenue which has been transformed by the magic of the painter João Abel Manta.

Azulejos are very much a part of the vocabulary of contemporary Portuguese architecture. In Lisbon Ana Maria Viegas employs painters who design azulejos specifically to match architectural requirements. She also displays some of their creations in her well-known gallery, the Galeria Ratton, established in 1987.

Innovation along with conservation—this was also the approach of the banker Ricardo do Espírito Santo Silva when, in 1953, he set up the foundation bearing his name, which he subsequently bequeathed to the Portuguese nation. A perceptive patron of the arts, he attempted to support and develop the skills of Portugal's artisans, which were in danger of dying out.

Conservation comes first for the Museum of Decorative Arts, established in a seventeenth-century palace in Alfama. Its treasures evoke faraway places: East India Company porcelain, family furniture in exotic woods with fabulous names, engraved silverware made from Brazilian ingots. But concern for continuing tradition is equally present in the form of some fourteen

workshops where master artisans practice the traditional crafts of delicate cabinet-making, carving, and lacquering. Commissions come from all over the world.

Innovation best describes the School of Arts and Crafts, and the School of Decorative Arts, breeding grounds for future artists. As magicians of Portuguese art, students learn to innovate without making a *tabula rasa* of tradition.

Lisbon is a tumult of creativity that somehow manages to stay in check. If one's memory could retain only one image of this city, it would probably be a vision of the Tagus. The river has an extraordinarily powerful presence—whether glimpsed through the phenomenal marble triumphal arch in praça do Comércio, or contemplated as its blue waters are framed between a fragrant jasmine bush and the yellow ochre walls of some ancient Bairro Alto palace. At one moment it is gray. You look away, thinking you hear a foghorn, then turn back, and it is all light. This fabulous river seems to sum up all the beauties of a wonderful city.

People come from all around the world to buy Portugal's handmade goods. The most renowned are the silverware produced in Lisbon for Tiffany's in New York, the huge Arraiolos carpets embroidered for immense palaces, and fine tablecloths created by skillful hands for royalty and world leaders—not to mention the furniture and *objets d'art* made in the workshops of the Espírito Santo Foundation. Seventeen traditional crafts are represented in these celebrated workshops (top and right).

The amazing Solar Albuquerque e Sousa, the country's most renowned seller of antique azulejos, was established in 1957 by José Manuel Leitão. The marvelous collection, organized by time period, is being continued by his son Manuel Leitão. One is struck by the vigor of the designs and the fantastic freshness of the high-fired colors, especially the copper greens, cobalt blues, antimony yellows, and manganese violets. Individual azulejos or complete assembled panels can be purchased (bottom left and far right).

The Alentejo

The vast horizons of the Alentejo landscape unfold before your eyes. Dotted with ancient olive groves and row after row of cork oaks, this region becomes a blaze of color in springtime (preceding double page).

Is Portugal really such a small country? When looking at the immensity of the Alentejo such an assumption seems impossible. *Além Tejo* "beyond the Tagus" is a region of huge plains with rolling hills that stretch out to infinity—an unbounded land that is easy to love.

It is winter, the cold is settling in, the wind blows, and the earth is brown. The melancholy of the landscape is somewhat assuaged by the gray of immense skies—a paradox expressed in another way by thousands of olive trees with gnarled trunks but light, silvery foliage. However the abandoned impression given by this countryside is illusory. The Alentejanos are harvesting the fruit of the trees that give precious olive oil. Smoke from burners making charcoal rises in the distance. Sometimes the chirping of birds and the grunting of wild boars can be heard. And in sheltered orchards, fragrant orange and lemon trees bow under the weight of their fruit.

When spring arrives the rolling landscape becomes a whirling eddy, with colors that suggest a

The writer Miguel Torga evoked the Alentejo with a burning intensity: "Nothing moves me so much as an ocean of land that is bare, austere, and virile. . . . In other provinces you no longer see the earth, because it is covered with a domestic vegetation that is already more than eight centuries old, or because erosion has stripped the flesh from its body and left only the bones. But the land of Alentejo can still be gazed upon in its original virgin state, open and exposed. And that is what moves me to the core." (On these two pages: the Alentejo countryside in spring).

A typical Alentejan house, with its high chimney and outbuildings (middle and bottom).

Flocks of sheep living out in the open, bulls that will fight in the ring, and black pigs are found scattered throughout the solitude of the vast spaces (far left and top).

fireworks display. The violet of alfalfa flowers, the red of poppies, the tender green of new grass, the white petals of rock roses make up a picture that is almost psychedelic. The days are growing longer, and the shepherds, protected by their *safões,* a traditional garment lined with sheepskin, watch over their newborn lambs. Storks are already nesting on the church towers.

How could the Alentejo be labeled a monotonous province? In the heat of summer, the vast gilded landscape, shining like platinum gold, really comes into its own. In the *campos,* or fields, farmers harvest the wheat, which is the symbol of this land. To the south, the towering silhouettes of combine harvesters stand out against the infinite horizon. Rows of women can still sometimes be seen working in the fields with their skirts tucked up between their legs, and black felt hats perched on top of their headscarves. Elsewhere, in the vast cork oak forests, precious bark is being harvested from thousands of trees. Their trunks turn brilliant red when the bark is stripped, then become darker, a fading shriek of color. Birds fly wildly in the dust. At dusk the air gradually cools down. As the heat haze disappears, another landscape reveals itself beneath a clear night sky, lit by the moon and sparkling with stars, as in the desert.

There are no fences, no hedges, and no furrowed lanes in the Alentejo. In autumn, far in the distance, you see tremendous flocks of sheep or black pigs ranging free—as in the Middle Ages—rooting peacefully for acorns and sometimes digging up white truffles. As Miguel Torga said: "The land of Alentejo can still be appreciated in its original state, virgin, open, and exposed. . . . Here perhaps a being can still touch the clay from which God created it."

A chapel near Monsaraz—an interplay of light and color on what seems to be a white vessel floating in the immensity of the plain (following double page).

DAZZLING WHITE TOWNS AND VILLAGES

From north to south, to travel through the Alentejo is an endless source of pleasure. Sometimes, at the top of a hillock, a few isolated white houses appear. These *montes* are landmarks of the agricultural terrain and distantly related to Roman villas. At the start of the century prominent local families, both Portuguese and English, built the functional, welcoming *montes* that house the workers of vast estates. Days are hard during the harvest but in the evening when the work is done, poignant strains of song can sometimes be heard—the sound of day laborers singing in the night.

Alentejo is the realm of wheat and olives. Until the beginning of this century the local wines were not particularly esteemed. However, in recent years the vineyards have become more developed. The possibilities of these regional wines are now such that important companies such as the Domaines Barons de Rothschild (Lafite) estate represented by Eric de Rothschild have taken an interest. Among these wines one might cite the reds and whites of the Borba region, of which the best are perhaps those of the Quinta do Carmo, originating in the rocky land near Estremoz. The wines of Évora come principally from the large Herdade de Cartuxa estate. The areas of Reguengos de Monsaraz, Vidigueira, and Moura also produce very good wines.

As if out of respect for the land, the towns and fortified villages, with their long histories—such as

Overlooking the plain, Monsaraz is one of Portugal's most beautiful villages. While the eye alone cannot immediately take in the range of things to be seen, photography succeeds in capturing them at all levels (top, middle, and right).

In this fine light a simple window becomes a work of art (Estremoz, bottom).

Pastelaria
A
Cisterna

The old town of Monsaraz, near the Spanish border, has been miraculously preserved through all the sieges, invasions, assaults, and looting that it has suffered. To stroll through its streets is a source of constant delight. At every step you find a church, a chimney, walls rippling in the light, an interesting angle, or an unusual perspective. Sometimes the immensity of the plain below suddenly reveals itself through a gateway in a wall. In a sense the walls have stopped time, and within their span you see a Gothic portal, a Manueline gemel window, a seventeenth-century wrought-iron balcony, a baroque steeple—the volumes unified by dazzling white. The whiteness, an expression of a whole culture, contrasts with the roughness of slabs of sombre gray schist lying on the ground (left).

Everywhere in the Alentejo, handsome doorways stand out from immaculate white walls. The door arches often have complex, trefoil shapes, as above.

Portuguese women have always been particularly skilled at embroidery (bottom).

Évora leaves an extraordinary impression on the visitor, as a town which has survived the centuries. Its history is continually being inscribed in stone, whether on granite tinged with gold by the years, whitewashed walls, or cream and pink marble. In the town's twisting alleys and on its large squares unending perspectives and an incredible variety of monuments appear—Roman columns, medieval ramparts, the cathedral, monasteries, and palaces (top).

Évora, Estremoz, Vila Viçosa, or Portalegre—stand on hills at some distance from each other. Each time they appear is an enchantment, particularly Évora, the most beautiful town in Alentejo. It provides a true voyage through the Portuguese imagination, with a Roman temple, openwork balconies, Moorish patios and hanging gardens, medieval walls and cathedral, Manueline gemel windows, and Renaissance atlantes side by side with modern sculptures by João Cutileiro. An astonishing unity has been created within constantly changing diversity. Perhaps the best way to understand the subtlety of the Portuguese way of life is to visit Évora. The nights of the Alentejan summer, when the air is sweet and the stars are bright, are the ideal time to walk and simply let yourself be consumed by the magic of the place.

In towns such as Évora, Estremoz, Vila Viçosa, Portalegre, Arraiolos, Monsaraz, and Marvão, Alentejo represents the triumph of white. And this is equally true in the humblest of villages. Is the white there merely as a defense against the summer heat? Or is white—as the architect Antonio Teixeira Guerra, a native of the region, suggests—a symbol, a way of appropriating and humanizing an often hostile nature, an action of domination through which a culture is expressed? People are endlessly whitewashing walls and even stairways with brushes fixed to the ends of long poles or with antiquated spraying machines. It is even said that a hat left hanging on a wall can be inadvertently whitewashed by the time you return for it!

Forged by this open terrain, which is free of enclosures, the Alentejano is a lone individualist, a man of infinite dignity. As a free man, he keeps his hat on his head even when he is talking with others (at Monsaraz, right). In the sun-scorched streets the children also wear straw hats (bottom).

The chimneys of the Alentejo are always surprising, due to their height. Here we see twin sisters (far right, top).

In Portugal window frames are often edged with bright colors (far right, bottom).

In the villages the houses are low and simple with few openings in order to protect the interior from both heat and cold. The chimneys are particularly impressive, since they are most often taller than the houses themselves. Generally huge and rectangular, each is nearly always different, repeating like slow beats on the horizon.

The white walls, contoured by the light, are never boring. Sometimes they are given rhythm by adding color, with a typically Portuguese simplicity marked by elegance. The ochres, indigo blues, bull's-blood reds, and greens that appear at the corners of house fronts, cornices, and window frames are true marvels. In the town of Redondo, a broad azure-blue band painted across the corner of a modest home is as worthy of dreams as the sumptuous polychrome pilaster with Corinthian capital of a neighboring house—a remarkable and noble simplicity.

What an extraordinary land where, from the heights, ramparts of brown stone open through narrow posterns onto white towns. Castelo de Vide, cooled by the Serra de São Mamede, is known as the Sintra of Alentejo. In this harmonious town, which is full of surprises, the neighborhoods of Arçário and Judiaria offer the finest collection of Gothic portals in Portugal. The fonte da Vila is truly magical; the sound of its running water alone seems to fill the surrounding space (left and bottom).

At Évora, in the large Portas de Moura square, this famous Renaissance fountain illustrates the new vision of the world that arose with Copernicus's discoveries on the movement of planets in the solar system. In the background stands the Casa Cordovil (top).

Life in the Alentejo is also the art of making the best use of water, often a rare commodity in the region. There are fountains everywhere. At Castelo de Vide, an astonishing town that has remained intact over the centuries, nearly three hundred can be counted. The most splendid is the fonte da Vila, with its Renaissance marble columns, standing at the center of the town's steep little streets. The fountains have become less important as meeting places since piped water was introduced, but they have continued to play an important social role—the reason so much care was applied to their construction. All sorts of fountains can be found, from marble to more rustic whitewashed materials. Their lines are always pure—a sphere at Évora, a colonnade at Alter do Chão, a pyramid and a cylinder at Monsaraz. Sometimes, as at Arraiolos, it may be a simple wall enlivened by scrolled decoration in yellow or blue. Such elegance with such an economy of means is yet another of Alentejo's secrets, a secret one finds as a kind of leitmotif in the interiors of all its residences.

In Alentejo the countryside is never far away, which accounts for the importance of the region's markets. That of Estremoz, known throughout the region, takes

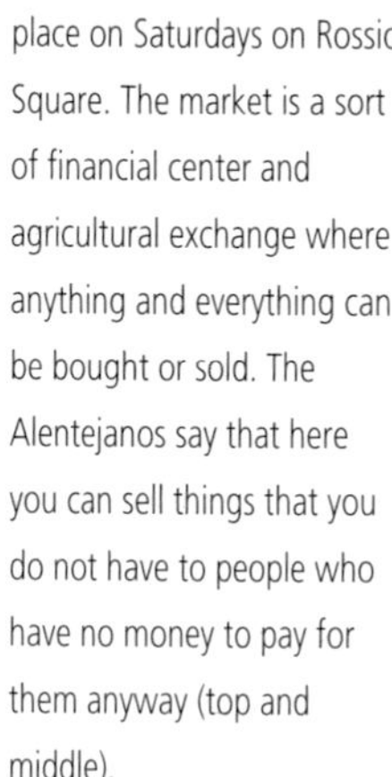

place on Saturdays on Rossio Square. The market is a sort of financial center and agricultural exchange where anything and everything can be bought or sold. The Alentejanos say that here you can sell things that you do not have to people who have no money to pay for them anyway (top and middle).

"If a man is truly wise, he can sit on a chair and enjoy the spectacle of the whole world." Fernando Pessoa, *The Book of Disquiet* (far right).

Here you can still find the characteristic *carros de canudo*, small carts that are sometimes tarpaulin-covered (below, at Borba).

In Alentejo people gather not only around fountains, but also in market places. The Estremoz Saturday market, the huge popular market of Évora in June, or that of Castro Verde in mid-October are among the most picturesque. The Alentejanos still often wear traditional costume, while women wear black. They arrive from the surrounding villages early in the morning, some of them riding in small, heavily laden carts pulled by donkeys. Here you find *capotes,* loose-fitting greatcoats with fox-fur collars worn by shepherds, and the extraordinary Nisa embroidered felt, made up of fabric appliqués, used as insertions in tablecloths and cushions. Stalls are piled with multicolored blankets called *mantas* woven at Reguengos de Monsaraz. Further along, pottery is spread out on the ground or displayed in stacks. The most striking aspect of these markets is the noble bearing of the Alentejanos, who carry within them all the dignity of this free and unfenced land.

10

In the region's vast expanses the houses, with white walls pierced by only occasional openings, are organized around patios enlivened by fountains. They are designed to be cool and agreeable despite the intense heat which governs the area for a good part of the year. The astonishing crop of chimneys, on the other hand, is explained by the rigors of winter. Frescoes and azulejos on the inside of the houses contrast with the austerity of the exteriors. The people of this proud and noble province know how to create living spaces, both humble and splendid, where the lifestyle manages to combine both grandeur and simplicity.

A PALACE WITH A PLACE IN HISTORY. Évora has survived over centuries. Roman and Visigoth walls, Mudéjar-style arched windows, Italian-style loggias and frescoes all bear witness to this. Because of its long history, Miguel Torga dreamed of requiring every Portuguese person to take a retreat in Évora. The palace of the counts of Basto, where Dom Sebastião often stayed, is found here. The Portuguese are still awaiting the glorious return of the "longed-for king" who disappeared suddenly while he was fighting the Moors at Alcácer-Quibir in 1578. For the poet Fernando Pessoa, the mysterious phenomenon of "Sebastianism," the dream of a providential savior, might have even been inherent in the Portuguese soul since the beginning of time.

In this superb palace, the interlinking rooms are vaulted and decorated with frescoes in the Italian style. The king must have sat here and contemplated his conquests, as he gazed at frescoes depicting a battle in North Africa. Closer to our own time, the count and countess of Vill'Alva have worked to preserve the charm of this historic residence, while at the same time playing an important role in the city life of Évora. The late count, who had a builder's disposition, was actively involved in the reestablishment of the university of

The shades of blue and ochre that emphasize the region's architecture are truly wonderful. Here they provide a counterpoint to the scrolled contours of a pediment (left).

At Évora the residence of the counts of Basto is one of the most important sixteenth-century palaces in Portugal, representing the town's period of glory. In the interior several vaulted rooms are decorated with tempera painting. Here the motifs are characteristic Renaissance trophies and birds (top right).

Évora. During the difficult period of the 1974 revolution he also set up the Eugénio de Almeida Foundation. The institute offers research scholarships, contributes to the maintenance of the immense palace, and manages major land resources, including a prestigious vineyard to the south of Évora on the road to Reguengos de Monsaraz. Under the appellation Herdade de Cartuxa, its excellent red and white wines, stored in superb wine lodges adjoining the Cartuxa or "Carthusian" monastery, have taken numerous prizes. The very fullness of these popular wines reveals much about the character of this original land.

A Horse-rearing Estate. Évora is also horse country, as we were shown by João Fiuza da Silvera on his family farm, the Herdade da Pereira. This typically low-built house, whitewashed and edged with blue, is topped by an immense chimney. The entrance is flanked by a colonnaded portico, and the geometry of its capitals, highlighted in blue, is a joy to behold. The interior houses precious collections of pewter, copperware, and East India Company porcelain that have been handed down from generation to generation. An early eighteenth-century carved-wood shrine, in the style of Dom João V, opens onto statues of saints displayed before a flowered

Table presentation is an art in this noble residence: the handsome glass service sets off red and white wines of Herdade de Cartuxa, coming from the vineyards of the house (top left and bottom right).

A reliquary, religious pictures, and saints' images show a personal devotion, a pious tranquillity, almost surprising in this grandiose setting (bottom left).

Exotic woods, lacework, and azulejos at the Quinta do Carmo (top).

The Herdade da Pereira house near Évora still maintains a bedroom with a fine slatted wooden ceiling and painted décor. Garlands of flowers and foliage are executed delicately in the Dona Maria I style (bottom).

The palace and gardens of the Quinta do Carmo are splendid. From a grand esplanade enclosed by walls, a classical portal opens onto a second garden, also enclosed. Here a dense vegetation spreads around covered walkways that seem to tunnel through the greenery. There is a superb contrast between the balanced symmetry of the columned portal and the exuberant freedom of nature (far right).

trompe l'oeil brocade. Such oratórios testify to a family tradition of piety that is very Portuguese, at once personal and social. In the office a composition by the sculptor João Cutileiro seems to summarize the immense Alentejano plain, to which he gives life and movement with a combination of ochre red marbles, veined with black and white, alternated with blueish grays.

On his stud farm, João Fiuza da Silveira rears thoroughbred Lusitanian horses bearing the brand Casa Fiuza F, which are lively, pleasant, intelligent, and from a breed similar to the horses that were once ridden by the kings of France. They are used for bullfighting, riding, teamwork, and hunting—all disciplines enthusiastically pursued by the family. Since the estate holds an abundance of hares, the lord of the manor, following British tradition, organizes famous hare hunts several times a year. It is a fast-moving scene of great beauty, as he rides out with a few fellow horsemen and his pack of fifty dogs. Afterwards they gather in the large hunting room to give homage to the region's gastronomy. During the season, game stew *favada de caça* or jugged hare *chanfana de lebre* are feasted upon. In Alentejo the cuisine is particularly aromatic. Garlic and especially fresh coriander—a distant reminder of the long Moorish presence—are much used, particularly for delicious rustic soups, in which bread is one of the principal ingredients. Thus, for example, *açorda alentejana* employs stock, a poached egg, garlic, coriander, and bread in a savorous blend. There is also *gaspatcho alentejano,* a traditional soup that workers take to the fields in cork thermos flasks called *tarros,* since in summer the soup is eaten well-chilled. Onions, cucumbers, tomatoes, and peppers are cut into very thin strips and mixed with oil and garlic. Bread is not only used in the making of soups; stale bread is also used with great art in all sorts of popular dishes known as *migas* or "breadcrusts." When cooked over a low flame with a little oil, it is also used as a sauce for meat or fish.

While João Fiuza da Silveira's friends savor these specialties, they discuss the forthcoming teamwork presentations. Following the example of the royal collections at the Lisbon Coach Museum, the Portuguese have always taken care to preserve their horse carriages. Here well-maintained Tilburies, Victorias, Carricks, and Phaetons show that the art of "driving" is very much alive.

THE QUINTA OF CLAY AND MARBLE. Life in Alentejo bears witness to a long-standing relationship between England and Portugal. Thus the famous Quinta do Carmo near Estremoz was handed down by the Reynolds, a leading English family in Alentejo, to their Portuguese cousins, the Bastos.

Julio Bastos, a very active person, shows us around the house and gardens of the estate's highly esteemed vineyards, under the management of the Bastos family and the Domaines Barons de Rothschild (Lafite) represented by Eric de Rothschild. On a single floor of the splendid palace Alentejano soil is found in its great variety of forms. Baked in an oven or dried in the sun, it is cut into slabs and glazed to tile floors; made into

In the kitchen of the Quinta do Carmo, the white vaulted ceiling, the red terra-cotta floor tiles, the blue-toned azulejos covering the walls, and the creamy-pink marble of the tables show that we are indeed in Alentejo. Here the care lavished on the décor of the kitchen, a very Portuguese trait, bears witness to the importance accorded to the art of cooking (left).

The charm of everyday things in the country (top, right).

In honor of his Spanish-born wife, a few years ago the father of the present owner had one room specifically dedicated to the art of bullfighting (bottom).

bricks and whitewashed it forms vaulted ceilings; cut into delicately glazed squares and decorated with cobalt paint it takes on the shape of azulejos.

The marvels of this residence include a splendid baroque cabinet of carved gilt wood displaying a porcelain service. The kitchen, for its part, is decorated with *avulso* azulejos, rustic tiles with individual motifs inspired by Delft azulejos that were imported in large numbers from the Netherlands during the eighteenth century. Marble is everywhere—in the rounded sink basins or *pias* as well as the large central table, both made of pink, cream-veined marble.

One of the curiosities of the residence, where it must be a pleasure to live, is a room dedicated to bullfighting mementos. Sitting on painted rustic chairs, the visitor can try local specialties served from glazed terra-cotta Estremoz bowls found in all the region's markets. And, of course, taste the excellent red and white wines of the Borba region that come from the Quinta do Carmo and are among the best in Portugal.

At Alvito, the Casa de Água de Peixes—the "Water of Fishes House"—where water flows in abundance is an oasis of coolness and poetry in the heat of the Alentejo (left).

There are Moorish reminiscences in this small-columned porch leading to a Manueline doorway (middle).

The countess Capodilista, who supervises untiringly the restoration of the fine Alentejo estate (above).

Surprising too are the gardens, which only reveal themselves in stages, as if by a process of initiation. The large enclosed esplanade gives way to a walled garden. A monumental portico gleams in the sun like a triumphal arch, then opens curiously into a tunnel of greenery, a dark grotto that leads into the Casa de Fresco. This cool pavilion is surrounded by walls lined with benches and potted flowers, and stands next to a huge basin that doubles as a swimming pool and water reservoir. This intimate space truly illustrates all of the culture of southern countries.

"Water of Fishes House." The Alentejo way of life is thoroughly impregnated with the centuries-long Moorish presence in Portugal. The Casa de Água de Peixes at Alvito is perhaps the most representative of their skill and refinement in the art of living. The very name "Water of Fishes House" evokes an oasis in the midst of an arid countryside.

Following Moorish custom, water flows into a huge basin, or *tanque,* that runs alongside the house. Use of the abundant water is carefully managed for irrigation of the estate. The early sixteenth-century architecture also shows the extent to which the Renaissance in Portugal was marked by the Moorish civilization of southern Spain. The austere walls present hardly any openings, except

It is as if air and light have been caught in the large courtyard with its imposing arcades and slender columns. A true garden of delights, fragrant with the scent of orange blossoms (top).

Here the upper gallery seems sculpted by the light (bottom).

for two windows framed by projecting arches. The brick-built gemel window and the corner window, a poetic marble mirador, have come to be, and remain, popular references throughout the country. Set off by the white walls stands an age-old olive tree that the owners, the count and countess Capodilista, succeeded in transplanting.

On the first floor, behind the panels of a Manueline door, all the splendors of the true Casa de Água de Peixes appear. A typically southern house, it is entirely turned toward the inner courtyard. The count and countess Capodilista have restored the patio with arches on the ground floor and an upper gallery on the first floor. The countess is currently continuing the work begun by her husband, restoring the chapel and the vast rooms.

As the guests gather in the dining room for an elegant meal by evening light, the handsome windows framed by horseshoe, or Moorish, brick arches become a fantastical evocation of the land of *The Thousand and One Nights*. Further on, beneath the arcade, enormous terra-cotta jars in which lime is stored bring to mind the ones in Ali Baba's treasure cave.

In a bedroom of Casa de Água de Peixes, the high ceiling virtually doubles the size of the room and contributes to the general sense of harmony. A bed in the Dom João V style adds to the room's charm (left).

A corner window features Manueline decorative elements (top).

The violet imitation marble skirting and the blues of the borders go wonderfully well with the multiple tones of iridescent creamy white throughout the bathroom (right).

The air is mild, the heat has lifted, and we sit in the upper gallery surrounding the courtyard. The freshness of the potted plants, the scent of orange blossoms, and the water murmuring nearby give this residence the air of an enchanting oasis.

A DÉCOR OF CARPETS AND FRESCOES. Another very refined house is the comfortable Casa Leal, at Reguengos de Monsaraz. In the summer, when the light is dazzling, one appreciates the coolness of its main hall. However, the presence of a large copper brazier is a reminder that winters can sometimes be harsh. A grand staircase leads up to the first floor. Here Maria do Carmo Sousa Uva receives us in a suite of very classically elegant rooms. However we soon realize that the inspiration for this house is something else. The warm breadth of its proportions is like an echo of the vast spaces of the Alentejano countryside, while the vaulted ceilings recall traditional skills inherited from the Moors. And finally, the frescoes on the walls are very typical of the region, with its dry climate. Dating from the nineteenth century, they seek neither to enlarge the space nor to tell of noble deeds, as was the case in previous centuries. Here most of the main panels are bare, painted in light colors with decoration being limited to doorframes, paneling, window frames, and cornices. The lady of the house commissioned immense embroidered Arraiolos carpets in order to create a harmony with the décor. Indeed, one of the great pleasures of life in Portugal is to choose a workshop, discuss sizes and patterns, and choose from among the multiple shades of colors.

During sunny winter days and summer evenings it is a delight to be outside. In the courtyard, as well as on the grand terrace, you find motifs that are painted in a very Alentejan interpretation of the grammar of interior decoration. Here bougainvillaeas blend with white columns, of which the fluting is set off in creamy ochre. An almost *trompe l'oeil* entablature presents an interplay of bands, friezes, and stripes that runs the

Built more than three hundred years after the Casa de Água de Peixes, the Casa Leal illustrates a totally different conception of architecture. Here the walls have a decoration that seeks quite simply to delight the eye. In the dining room their ochre tones are in harmony with the colors of the table cloth, the Arraiolos carpet, and the Nisa embroidered door curtains. On the grand terrace, by *trompe l'oeil* effect, artistically arranged plants in Medici vases provide a counterpoint to the burgeoning vegetation (above and right).

The awakening of Monsaraz reflects a region that is rediscovering itself without renouncing a certain past. In this spirit Mizette Nielsen and Gilles Kalisvaart have restored several houses here. The guesthouse reserved for friends, with a staircase built into the stonework and reed ceiling is wholly typical of the region (above).

gamut of a decorative grammar derived from neoclassicism. And the creamy ochres, like a magic potion, seem to concentrate onto a wall shaped by human hands all of the Alentejo vastness at the hour of the setting sun.

An Artists' Domain. One of the pleasures of Monsaraz, whether morning or evening, is to admire the reflections of the sun as it falls on the surrounding countryside. Mizette Nielsen and her husband Gilles Kalisvaart have settled here, bringing several old houses back from a state of dilapidation, opening a shop, and setting up their own home. The austere schist sculptures of Gilles Kalisvaart stand out against the whitewashed interior—a synthesis of an Alentejo that the artist has continuously sought to uncover during his long hunts across the land. Always busy, Mizette Nielsen has managed to reproduce a décor which is very typical of the region. She also directs a workshop in Reguengos de Monsaraz, one of the last of its kind, which uses old looms to make the region's traditional *mantas*—rug-blankets dating back to the sixteenth

A tall, wide, rectangular chimney towers above the house where Mizette Nielsen and Gilles Kalisvaart live. In the past the hearth was used to cook and smoke savorous meats from the famous Alentejo pork that the gastronomic journalist, Hipólito Raposo considers to be the world's best (bottom).

The interior is very simply furnished: a wooden table, straw-seated chairs, and a bench painted with tiny rustic flowers (right: top and bottom).

In the bedroom the bed is integrated into the house's architecture (far right).

century. Wool is dyed in bright colors, which are emphasized with black and brown. A marvelous artisanal creation, the wool yarn seems to echo the prodigious variety of the countryside, which is not in the least monotonous.

On the same looms Mizette also weaves Alentejan *trapos,* popular colored rugs produced with cotton scrap. These traditional rugs were originally designed to recycle fabric from old clothes.

Be it in town or in some *monte* out in the countryside, the guest is always welcome in this region with its wide-open spaces. In summer the Alentejanos offer the coolness of their houses, and during the hunting season the warmth of a wood fire. Above, the Casa de Peixinhos at Vila Viçosa.

Estremoz, a town with a thousand faces, is the location of the sumptuous Pousada da Rainha Santa Isabel. From its setting in the upper town it is reflected in the waters of the lower town. Meals here are served in a very pleasant dining room (above and bottom right).

CHÂTEAU LIFE IN A POUSADA

The Alentejo deserves a long stay to absorb the limitless landscapes, discover the power of the architecture, and try to make time stand still. A warm welcome is always assured and there are a number of choice places to stay. The finest are undoubtedly the palaces and old monasteries that have been turned into *pousadas*.

Pousar means simply to stop, come to rest, settle in. Like *paradores*—similar institutions in Spain—*pousadas* are created and managed by the state and are a wonderful way of discovering Portugal's most select sites. Some of these charming hotels have been created in historic buildings remodeled by leading architects such as Fernando Távora. Others are located in more recent establishments where the architecture draws on local traditions. All of them provide opportunities to discover Portugal in all the passionate diversity of its landscapes and historical cities.

Cuisine also contributes to the experience, making each visit a discovery of Portuguese gastronomy. As for interior decoration, whether rustic or luxurious it is most often an attempt to recreate the ambience of a specific era or region. In one *pousada* the beds are of solid oak, in another of precious exotic woods, while in a third they are decorated with delicate painted motifs.

At the Pousada da Rainha Santa Isabel in Estremoz, the marble monumental staircase summons up an image of arriving royalty in bygone days. It is

There are many delightful places to stay in Alentejo. Right, the Quinta do Monte dos Pensamentos near Estremoz; bottom, the Casa dos Arcos at Vila Viçosa.

The Pousada dos Loios in Évora is truly a jewel. For unforgettable dining the restaurant has been set up in the former cloister (below).

perhaps here that one really understands that everything is grand in Alentejo. The vaulted dining room is immense; the landscape seen through the windows extends further than the eye can see; even the furniture here is impressive. In both the salons and the bedrooms, the mainly antique tapestries, the fine four-poster beds, carved-wood cabinets, and chests of drawers give each guest the impression of having been there forever.

In Évora the Pousada dos Loios has other surprises in store. Here too a décor of baroque frescoes and antique furniture contributes to a general sense of harmony. After a swim in the pool built at the center of the patio, the most enjoyable moment is perhaps dinner in the vaulted Manueline cloister. The beauty of the marbles in the chapter house, of the gemel windows, and the monks' washbasin where the water gently murmurs, mixes perfectly with the quality of the food.

In addition to the *pousadas* certain other delightful residences accept paying guests. The Quinta do Monte dos Pensamentos in Estremoz is a one-time *monte,* which until recently functioned as a hunting lodge. Its small turrets in the Moorish fashion are an invitation to travel further south. In this comfortable house the guest discovers with rapture the depth of the Portuguese attachment to ceramics. Displayed on the walls is a collection of

more than five hundred faïence plates, giving all of the rooms an endless charm. Some come from factories in northern Portugal. Others, of popular inspiration, were brought from the Coimbra region by Ratinhos—men from the Beiras province who did seasonal work in Alentejo and lived together in the *montes.*

Another select place to stay is the impressive Convento de São Paulo monastery near Estremoz in the middle of the Serra de Ossa. Since the sites of the Alentejo are so beautiful, they often become the decisive factor in deciding where to stay. The Convento de São Paulo monastery is perhaps chosen for its remote location, the beauty of the landscape, or the memory of members of the royal family having stayed there. It is possibly here that one finds the happiest alliance of marble, clay, and frescoes—the basic elements of this province's architecture. First marble, which

has been used for the sumptuous staircase, the basins that joyfully overflow with mountain spring water, and the bathrooms. Clay, for its part, has here been enameled to produce azulejos on which entire biblical stories, repeated dozens of times, unfold down the length of the corridors. These scenes were painted in shades of blue by the best artists of the first half of the eighteenth century. Finally, the frescoes, which enliven the former refectory transformed into an elegant dining room. In this delightful setting you can sample *carne de porco alentejana,* a striking combination of casseroled clams and filleted pork that every restaurant prepares in its own way.

In summer, when it is very hot, the Casa de Peixinhos at Vila Viçosa appears with its ramparts and looks like a mirage. However its pleasures are real. The lady of the house receives her guests in a peaceful white-painted residence that has been remodeled over the years and is now trimmed with dazzling ochres. The unforgettable fragrance of orange blossom perfumes the night.

The luxurious Convento de São Paulo near Redondo is also a select place to stay. The corridors here are decorated with splendid azulejos (top). Tucked back into the hillside, the patio is a haven of coolness. The architecture here is in constant movement, as in the scrolled borders of the azulejos and the impressive stone framing devices that decorate the fountain (right).

The dining room is decorated with azulejos and frescoes (bottom).

Why continue making terra-cotta jugs and pitchers that are heavy and easily broken, when plastic containers are light and unbreakable? This is the challenge to which the artisans of Alentejo must rise. However their creations, more functional than one might think, are beautifully conceived. These jugs, for example, have the ability to keep water deliciously cool (left, top and bottom).

Estremoz was already making *bonecos* (figurines) at the end of the eighteenth century. These little statues, pure marvels of popular art, are made out of clay, and therefore cost less than the carved wooden statues which inspired them. Today subject matter still consists of characters from everyday life, but also nativity and allegorical figures. Their charm derives from a combination of precisely observed detail and a slightly delirious imagination. Size varies according to the model, and may be anything from two inches to two feet high for a Virgin Mary or figures of saints such as Saint John and Saint Anthony (bottom right).

Again in Vila Viçosa, the Casa dos Arcos welcomes its guests in the summer season in its loggia, or on the patio, under a marble arcade that evokes the splendors of the Italian Renaissance. A stay here gives an opportunity to taste some fine ewes'-milk cheese. The Évora cheese, also known as *queijinho d'Alentejo,* is sometimes preserved in olive oil. The best known of these cheeses is *serpa,* which is strong and slightly tangy. Its crust, brushed during the maturing process with olive oil and paprika, has a brick-colored tinge.

QUALITY ARTS AND CRAFTS

A stay in Alentejo also permits the discovery of the most active artisanal tradition in Portugal. The first stop could be at Azaruja, a village lying at the heart of the cork-oak forests. Here, as do some dozen other artisans, Joaquim Correia Pereira sits by a pile of bark in his small workshop. First he soaks the bark, flattens it and smoothes it. Then he uses it to make *tarros*—efficient rustic thermos flasks—or to carve spoons, bowls, and other surprising objects.

Nisa, Estremoz, Redondo, São Pedro do Corval, and Reguengos de Monsaraz are the realms of pottery production. The region's hot climate led to the making of recipients to keep water cool by using as raw material the clay often found in the earth at one's feet. In these pottery workshops, which are called *olorias,* the work is still done on a family basis. At São Pedro do Corval there are still nearly sixty potters whose craft skills have been

At Estremoz, Redondo, Reguengos de Monsaraz, São Pedro do Corval, and Nisa craft workers produce red clay pottery, either matte, or glazed and painted with naïve motifs. The craft has always been kept in the family, with the potter generally working on his own, helped by his wife and children.

passed down from father to son. The Filhão family, for example, has been operating out of their workshop for almost four hundred years. They use a wheel to produce pottery that is then glazed in pale yellow and decorated with traditional floral motifs. In the gloom at the back of the workshop sit stacks of pottery that, as if by magic, is made of a fragile, perishable material in shapes as old as the world itself.

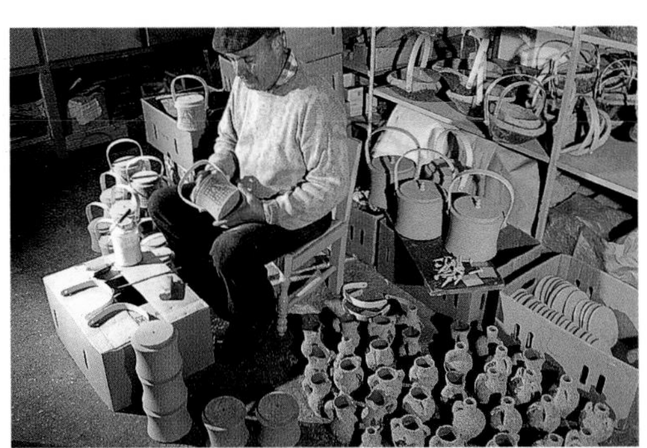

It is the ceramics produced in the town of Estremoz—the *púcaros,* jugs of Arabic origin in very fine red clay, decorated with white stones—which have long been Portugal's most famous form of pottery. There was even a time when flavored clay was used to produce small *púcaros* that noble Portuguese ladies apparently nibbled with pleasure once they had drunk the contents.

Today the finest ceramics produced in Estremoz are the area's famous figurines, the *bonecos.* Originally the workshops made small clay figures for Christmas, focusing on nativity scenes and religious figures. Then they began to take their inspiration from everyday life, creating figures based on the local gentry, such as the lady of the *monte,* or on ordinary country people, shepherds, and so on. These naïve and gracious statuettes, painted in bright colors—made by the Ginja brothers and the Flores sisters among

Alentejo is the land of cork. There is no shortage of raw material for the artisans, who have toiled in these workshops for many a year (bottom left).

In the Alentejo, since the sixteenth century women have woven *mantas* at home. These woolen blankets and rugs are of natural colors, brown or écru. Some dozens of years ago certain of these fabrics were still soaked in olive oil to make waterproof clothing for use by shepherds. Here we see the hand looms in the workshop set up by Mizette Nielsen for weaving traditional *mantas*. There is a choice of about seven colors, some of which are quite bright. Carpets, curtains, and bedspreads, are produced in the workshop (top, middle, and bottom).

The Arraiolos carpets that are the pride of every good Portuguese household seem to have been born in Alentejo. The first ones, embroidered onto linen canvas by women working either in their own homes or in convents, are close copies of Persian carpets. Later they drew on Indian and other motifs. Now the carpets are also embroidered in other regions (bottom right, detail of a bow embroidered on canvas).

An old-fashioned washstand: wrought iron, ceramic, and embroidered cotton (right).

Treasures are to be found in the museums of popular arts and crafts. In the Handicraft Museum at Evoramonte all the whiteness of Alentejo seems to be reflected on this tablecloth inundated with light. The wonderful embroidery work is also symbolic, as it spells out stitch by stitch the problems, doubts, and immense joys of everyday life (far right).

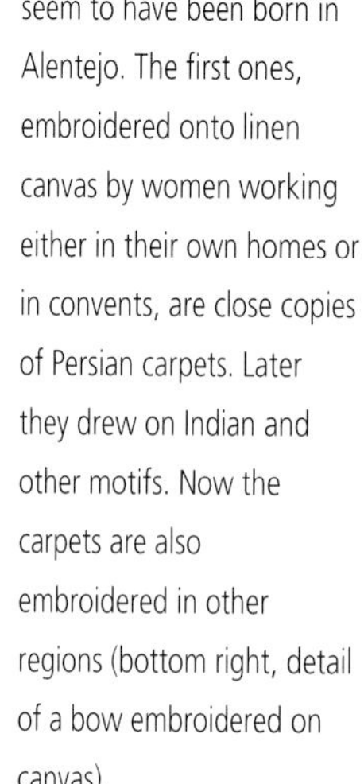

others—are perhaps among the most beautiful traditional craft creations in Portugal today.

As for carpets, those of Arraiolos are internationally famous. Arabic in origin, the first known examples of these embroidered carpets date from the start of the seventeenth century. In the village and surrounding area, either in workshops or at home, women cross-stitch embroider onto linen backing. The designs are traditionally drawn from Persian carpets, or from the Indo Portuguese motifs also found on Castelo Branco bedspreads. The carpets can be ordered from workshops in the area and can even be custom-made according to a specific motif.

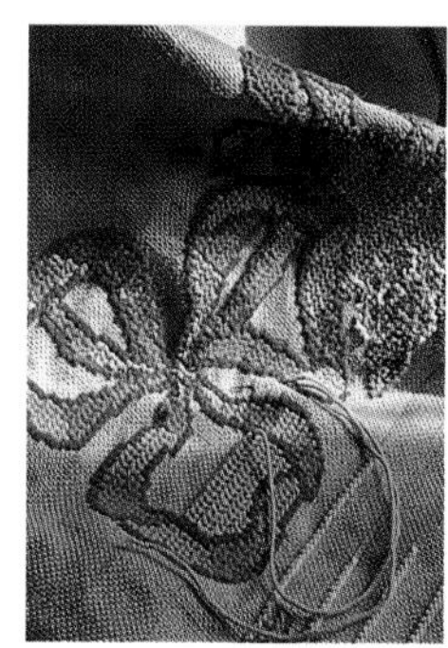

The Algarve

Portugal is a country of extraordinary diversity. After the poignant immensity of Alentejo, with its wheat fields, cork oaks, and olive trees, when you first see the Algarve from the heights of the do Malhão, do Caldeirão, and de Monchique *serras,* it looks like some amazing kingdom, a garden sheltered from the winds. The mountains, the plain, and the sea all contribute to the incomparable beauty of the region. You must also add, of course, the blue of the skies, the transparency of the air, the fabulous light, and the unique climate that makes it possible for Mediterranean plants to grow side by side with the vegetation of both temperate Europe and Africa. At Silves, in the time of the Muslim domination, the poet Ibn Said was already singing the praises of this garden—*al-Gharb*—meaning "the garden" or perhaps "the west." And today the Algarve continues to be a source of dreams outside the period of the regular summer rush toward the sun.

From the heights of the Serra de Monchique the traveler gazes out on the variety of this extraordinary landscape. The sea sparkles in the distance. The weather is mild. Waterfalls murmur, hot springs gush from the mountainside and water flows on all sides, irrigating the terraced fields. The green harmonies of light-filled meadows, pine forests, cork oaks, and chestnut trees echo each other. Sometimes bananas, figs, and yams are found growing in sheltered valleys. In springtime, Monchique is a blaze of color, with mimosas, azaleas, and narcissi all in bloom.

In Barrocal, between the mountain and the coast, lies the land of almond trees. Standing alone, in small clusters, or extending out of sight over vast fields, they stud the landscape with shades of white, pink, and lilac. Each winter the surprise is renewed. Legend has it that a Moorish emir's young wife—a melancholic northern princess—was pining away far from the snows of her own country. To make her smile again, her husband had a forest of almond trees planted around his palace. When January came, she was enthralled to find the hills covered with a great mantle of white. Men hiding in the trees shook the branches and snow seemed to fall to the ground. Thus in the Algarve winter it continues to snow almond blossoms!

All year long, in the valleys and plains, the Algarvios use ancient skills inherited from the Moors to transform this land into a *horta,* a flourishing garden. Here they grow onions, peas, tomatoes, and most particularly the broad beans used fresh in delicious local specialties. The hills are dotted with fruit-bearing trees: fig, olive, pomegranate, banana, orange, and lemon. The resplendent green of a golf course—in this region they are among the best in Europe—occasionally punctuates the landscape. And everywhere the heat, tempered by sea breezes, heightens the scent of fragrant jasmine and oleander bushes.

Here you are never far from the sea. Along the coastline there is a series of small, picturesque ports with multicolored boats. At Cacela Velha, Tavira, Fuseta, Armacão de Pêra, and Lagos everything recalls the epoch of the first

In Sotavento the sky has disappeared and the sea has invaded the countryside (at Cacela Velha, preceding double page). On this coast, from which so many navigators have set off, the poetry of Camões comes to mind: "Why do you pursue me, eternal *saudades*? With what hope are you tricking me again?"

The tawny-colored cliffs carved out by the sea, the emerald green of the water and the gold of the sandy beaches make Barlavento one of the finest coasts in Europe (right, Portimão).

"Praia da Rocha must be seen in winter, when all the tourist buses are gone and the daughters of Neptune again take possession of their watery kingdom," recommended Paul Morand. Here, strongly illuminated rocks, sculpted by the sea, are viewed from the pleasant Bela Vista hotel (top) and the Caniço restaurant, which was established by the celebrated interior decorator Maria José Salavisa (bottom).

caravels—boats that were modeled after the *caravo* of Arabic fishermen. To the east stretches a wild, flat coastline with lagoons called Sotavento, "leeward." The sky is reflected in calm waters; sand, dunes, moss, and reeds are infinitely delightful. Vast salt pans sparkle in the sun. In the huge marshland of the Castro Marim natural park a variety of rare aquatic plants are in full bloom. This is also the kingdom of birds—storks, pink flamingos, cattle egrets.

On the other hand, to the west, Barlavento, "windward," is much less wild. But this rocky coast is so beautiful that the real estate pressure has become almost pathetic. In Carvoeiro, or Praia da Rocha, or Ponta da Piedade, you need only take to the small paths or hire a boat to escape the crowds. As they reach out into the sea, the tawny, jagged, ochre rocks create arches, chaos, and magical grottoes. In the evening their amber color gives the shoreline that same gentle light that pervades certain Orientalist paintings by Delacroix or Ziem. At Ponta da Piedade there

In Sotavento, a flat, wild coastline extends between sand dunes that merge with the water and the music of the ocean under a never-ending sky (Cacela Velha, top).

At Olhão wooden posts driven into the sand compose a timeless landscape that would have no doubt inspired the painter Vieira da Silva (right).

From vantage points such as these one can imagine how people must have impatiently awaited the arrival of sailing ships, or watched anxiously as enemy ships came into sight (bottom).

A wonderful moment on the beach at Almacão de Pêra. At the day's end, the light reveals all the beauty of the Algarve beaches. Its magic enfolds the mauve sands and the blue nets, which are like light, ephemeral foam blown upon the beach (right).

Everywhere along the coast villages are dotted with multicolored boats. Anchored in the harbors, sometimes dancing to the rhythm of the tides, they make a wonderful spectacle. The bright primary colors, the variety with which tones are mixed, and the boats' naïveté all create an air of

irresistible gaiety that seems to be transferred to the vivid houses (top, Armacão de Pêra; bottom, Alcantarilha).

are marine grottoes where the fantastical outline of the rocks, the emerald of transparent waters, the green of the seaweed, the reddish brown of the cliffs, the iridescent light, and the gentle lapping of waves create an enchanting opera set.

Then, imperceptibly, at the Sagres Peninsula, the coastline begins to change again. It becomes harsh, inhospitable, even tragic. A shore without gentleness, a sea without serenity—is this the final destiny of the tormented continent of Europe? Is an alliance of opposites—gentleness and violence—one of the secrets of this kingdom? After all, this welcoming land is also the setting of the most heroic of exploits. It was from Sagres, a promontory lashed by the winds and waves, that in the fifteenth century the Infante Henry the Navigator prepared his maritime expeditions and sent his seamen and caravels out to unknown lands. These sailors drove back the horizon and extended the frontiers of the kingdom to infinity. They were the first to reach the Azores, sailing down the coast of Africa, round Cape Bojador and the Cape of Good Hope, before reaching the Indies and their precious spices.

"Portugal is an infinity of sea," murmured Fernando Pessoa as he contemplated their exploits. But the Age of Discoveries was followed by a long period of decline, an immense *saudade*. Five hundred years later, for Miguel Torga Sagres was only a "broken spirit, an arrow pointing to a road that has been lost in reality and symbolically . . . that could have become the departure point not so much for the impossible caravels of the past, but for the possible sailing ships of the present." Such anxiety is now no longer acceptable. The Portuguese have finally weaned themselves off "Sebastianist illusions, contemplative nostalgia, and flights of rhetoric."

Ferragudo watches over the estuary of the river Arade. Proudly built right at the water's edge, the port seems to submit to tidal invasions on stormy days. This superbly scenic fishing village is a maze of alleyways and stairs that climb up toward the church (left).

Albufeira is amazing. In 1250 it was the last stronghold in the Algarve to be conquered by the Portuguese. The town is still fighting back—but nowadays it battles against the more peaceful incursions of tourists. Its picturesque alleys preserve the traces of long-departed occupiers. Here, ancestral community links and the peace deriving from social solidarity are truly authentic (top).

Registros, small azulejo devotional panels placed on houses, are symbolic of a whole way of life. They usually represent the Virgin Mary or a patron saint (bottom).

WHITE TERRACES AND INTRICATE CHIMNEYS

In the Algarve, entryway to Europe and ancient land of communication with the Mediterranean countries, towns and villages still bear the stamp of the long Moorish presence. In this region with its face turned to the south, North Africa is never very far away. Discovering its little towns, so perfectly adapted to the climate and their environment, is a continual source of pleasure.

In the upper parts of Albufeira, streets that are narrow, sometimes vaulted, spanned by arches and cut across by stairs, provide welcome shade and coolness. The tiny windows of the houses, masked by slatted shutters, are so narrow that they barely permit the heat and light to enter. Here fishermen's wives prepare *arroz de langueirão,* an exquisite dish made with rice and razor clams. When the weather is fine and it is time to relax, people sit outside on stone benches or on the thresholds of their houses that open onto such welcoming narrow white streets.

Portugal's roofs, covered with Moorish tiles, have strikingly gentle lines. In Tavira houses individual rooms each have independent roofs, accounting for the inimitable grace of the multiple structures (bottom).

Olhão has all kinds of extraordinary buildings. Here columns and pilasters, classical statues and vases, stuccoes and ceramics construct a décor worthy of a palace in *The Thousand and One Nights* (far right).

Algarvios embellish everything in sight: star-patterned paving made out of basalt, sandstone, granite, and limestone; mule harnesses decorated by tassels with multicolored woolen pompons; delicate marzipans transformed into works of art, and the pediments of churches with ornamental stucco work (Olhão, top and middle).

The Moors have left their mark everywhere. Olhão is almost like being in Morocco. Outside staircases and terraces overlap, interlink, and superimpose on each other in an unstable equilibrium. The laws of perspective and interplay of volumes seem to be drowned out, annulled by the sparkling purity and the flashing white of the walls. This astonishing cubist village, which inspired one of Braque's collages, is bursting with life. Everywhere there are birds singing in cages among thousands of sundry rustic pots overflowing with lively vegetation. This is the land of *açoteias*—terraced roofs on which Algarvios dry fish, gather precious rainwater, come up to watch for boats at sea, and have wonderful dreams under the night sky. Like them, you would like to stay forever.

Tavira, one of the prettiest towns in the Algarve, also illustrates a lifestyle shaped by a long history. With its thirty-seven churches it seems to bristle with bell towers and chimneys, but also with cupolas and minarets that have Moorish antecedents. Graceful scissors-truss roofs cover the houses. These multiple roofs, known in Portuguese as *telhados de quatro águas,* "four water roofs," possibly had their origins in Africa or India—unless they arose simply from a choice to build lighter frameworks, since,

The cosmopolitan town of Faro preserves the beauty of its old town. A church tower welcomes the storks that come to nest in the Algarve (top).

It must take great skill to whitewash the surfaces of bell towers such as this. There is nothing more beautiful than the sight of white buildings standing out against the blue sky of the Algarve, unified in a single immaculate brilliance, with complex forms created by verticals, horizontals, diagonals, curves, and counter curves. The São Martinho d'Estói church illustrates a continuity of baroque forms with its bell tower surrounded by large ornamental vases (far right).

A woman, a cat, and a generously shady tree somehow seem to sum up the gentle Algarve lifestyle (bottom).

under this technique, each room has its own roof.

In the back country the villages are wilder and more secretive. Rising from the landscape are towns like São Brás de Alportel, or Caldas de Monchique, of which the waters are supposed to rejuvenate those who drink them. On the *serra,* the poetic market town of Monchique, with its steep alleys tumbling down the hillside and its terraces flowered by camellias, is like a garden of Eden. The fabulous light unveils a vast panorama that spreads from the mountains down to the sea on the horizon. The scent of mimosa hangs in the air. In this magical place every essence is brought together—those of the north mingling with those of the south. Even church towers and cornices provide a welcome for storks and swallows. From their workshops, and at the marketplace on the second Friday of the month, artisans sell all kinds of everyday objects made of wood, palm leaf, reeds, wicker, and ceramics. And every year all the farmers of this fertile region gather at the end of October for a grand fair, where the traditional rustic cuisine of the Algarve takes pride of place. Here an *ensopado de borrego* (mutton stew) or an *assadura de porco* (roast pork) take on a very particular flavor when they're washed down with a wine from Lagos, Portimão, Lagoa, or Tavira.

The Algarve is also light and heat, hence the dazzling white that protects the houses by reflecting the sun's rays. The usual technique is to use lime to cover walls that are made of pisé, rammed earth that makes an excellent insulator. The immaculate white of Alcantarilha is enhanced by the brightness of its flower-decked houses. Alte, tucked into the greenery with a rustic simplicity, seems to sprout directly out of the atmosphere, as if brought into being purely by the interaction of light and air.

In this smiling fertile land, which is a world away from the austere, harsh grandeur of its neighboring province, the architecture is adorned with a thousand nuances. The delicate

The picture helps to explain why Portuguese roofs have a characteristic gentle curve where they join the building. Since the walls are thick, roof eaves follow them horizontally before turning up (Cacela Velha, top).

Goats feeding by the sea at Cacela Velha bear witness to the double vocation of the Algarve as a land of both sailors and farmers (bottom).

chimneys of the Algarve contrast with the powerful structures of those in Alentejo. Each of these chimneys is the pride of its owner, and they are all different, the result of choice, even of inspiration. In Loulé, when a chimney is commissioned the artisan asks: "How many days do you want me to work on it?" According to inclination and the customer's purse, chimney's pop up constructed like lacework and finely ornamented—minaret, cupola, weathervane, jalousie, miniature bell tower, or dovecote—and always crowned with a variety of adornment. Loulé has a long craft tradition transmitted by the Moors. In the old Almedina quarter, you still find artisans beating copper, carving wood, working leather, and weaving rattan and willow.

Houses in the Algarve are generally built low. Thus their upper parts receive special attention, most likely to balance the proportions. This concern for harmony is the source of the balustraded balconies, entablatures, and stucco pediments. Nothing is ever systematic, because, as Paul Morand remarked, "the pediment is the necktie of façades, the frontispiece of these wide-open books. . . . Nowhere are whites harsher, shadows more blue, or reliefs more tortured than those that come to rupture these façades. Crowns, crosses, capital letters entwined in medallions, ovums, pearl moldings, sculpted corbels, garlands, and finials spread their stone jewels before the visitor's gaze."

On the whitewashed walls that act to diffuse the light, the color that underlines or defines the corners and angles of buildings becomes essential, even structural. Thus Lagos gives pride of place to blue, green, as well as ochre, and sometimes red and black. Doors and windows are often painted in bright colors. At Olhão you find the *tabuinhas*, partitioned wooden shutters, which also resound with the joys of this province.

When discovering the chapel of São Lourenço d'Almansil, near Faro, you understand the elation that becomes almost tangible in the Algarve, for the building is truly dazzling. The whole interior is entirely covered with wonderful azulejos. *Ad majorem dei gloriam.*

Such sweet nostalgia for another world fills the Algarve, particularly when the heat lifts. Then the nights reveal their powers of enchantment. Huge starry diamonds sparkle in a velvet sky. And when a full moon appears, towns and villages become magical places. Silves, the onetime Moorish capital, seems to relive its hours of glory, while age-old Faro, deserted and so brightly lit, has an incomparable charm. Terraces, patios, arbors, and pergolas then become marvelous places for rest and relaxation.

LIVING IN THE LAND OF THE SUN

The sun and sea make the Algarve a garden of Eden. The handsome old residences on the heights, and the modern summer houses on the coast, created by leading architects, invite the traveler to stop for a few days—or for a lifetime.

This fisherman's house is typical of Portugal's colors (right).

Buying fresh fish is one of the pleasures of the markets in the Algarve, where you find an abundance of ray, hake, mullet, and sardines. The fish sometimes have different names in Barlavento and Sotavento.

Here we see a large choice of cod in the market at Olhão (left and bottom).

The Algarve's markets are very lively. As a result of tourism the traditional crafts are tending to disappear, giving way to decorative

objects. This is often the case with items of saddlery, which sometimes end up as mountings for mirrors. The palm and wicker basketwork, traditionally woven by women, is still used for furniture, bags, and very fine mats. But the famous *bilhas*, the terra-cotta amphorae of Loulé, are increasingly rare. As for the *alcatruzes*—clay pots strung together that were once used to fetch up water on wheels—they are also used for octopus fishing (middle).

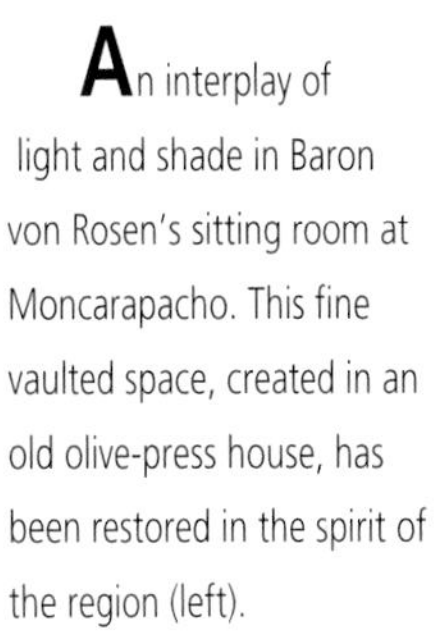

An interplay of light and shade in Baron von Rosen's sitting room at Moncarapacho. This fine vaulted space, created in an old olive-press house, has been restored in the spirit of the region (left).

The bedroom has a white-beamed wooden ceiling (top).

Small stone benches built within window corners were originally designed as pivot points for the wooden shutters (bottom).

THE HOME OF A WORLD CITIZEN. It was also the charm of the south that attracted Baron von Rosen to Moncarapacho near Fuseta. A scion of a very old Estonian family, he spent a long time looking for a place where he could recreate a lifestyle in the country, close to the land in the tradition of his ancestors. Finally this Baltic aristocrat, as a true citizen of the world, chose Portugal.

His estate, the Viveiro Monterosa, lies at the heart of one of the most fertile regions of the Algarve. In his superb nurseries, *ficus,* palm trees, and oleanders are cultivated either in a shady spot in the open or under glass. Baron von Rosen is one of the country's principal exporters of ornamental plants. In winter you should not miss a visit to the orchards, where trees bow beneath the weight of their fruit.

In this land of plenty, Baron von Rosen has chosen to live in an ancient olive-press house, from which, in the distance, one can see the sea. The façade appears to be pale ochre, earth having been mixed with the lime in order to lessen the

Christina von Rosen's charming house was formerly a small farm. Surrounded with greenery, the covered veranda provides a most agreeable spot (top).

dazzling effect of the white. In the interior, however, white predominates. The vaulted press house and its wooden ceilings have been restored in line with local tradition.

A Rustic House in the Land of Almond Trees. It was in this same spirit that Christina von Rosen, the Baron's sister, moved into an old house, the Casa Christina, near São Brás de Alportel. She could not have hoped to find a more beautiful place to settle than in this region where the mountains are blue and all the almond trees are covered with white winter blossoms.

Christina, who is artistic and very capable, has put a good deal of work into her house, which, as she says, now has a soul. The pleasantly proportioned rooms are decorated with charming rustic furniture from the surrounding area. Like her brother, the lady of the house is also undertaking the restoration of a former olive-press house, where she intends to set up a small cultural center dedicated to the region's cuisine, since Christina

Here, sitting in the shade, one can eat the traditional seafood *cataplana* and savor the *estrelas de figo*, pastries that combine the province's two most delicious fruits, figs and almonds (bottom).

Algarvios know how to embellish, ornament, and decorate with great attention to detail (far right).

Christina von Rosen loves to cook and she has created a cosy environment in her kitchen. A discreet Nordic touch recalls her origins (right).

is very fond of cooking. On her shady terrace, we sample the Algarve's most famous dish, delicious *ameijoas na cataplana*. It consists of clams that are simmered for a long time with smoked ham, loin of pork, and *chouriço* in a copper cooking vessel in the form of a double shell, which is probably of North African origin. The sea here is generous, and there are a number of other local specialties, based on seafood such as *berbigões* (cockles), *lapas* (limpets) and *burrié* (winkles).

Christina's latest creation, which is very typical of the Algarve, skillfully brings together figs, in the form of *aguardente de figo*, the region's famous fig liqueur, and, of course, almond paste—because in the Algarve, the kingdom of fruit and the land of almond trees, the almonds are of exceptionally good quality. *Queijinhos, castanhas, croquetes, palitos de amêndoa*—the names of all these sweets are barely translatable. These

There are very few noble manors in the Algarve, given a historical and social context that is very different to that of the north. The Fragoso house, which we see here viewed from the orchard, is all the more exceptional (left).

António and Bénédicte Fragoso have decorated their house with hundreds of charming objects gathered from all around the region. The *alcatruzes*—clay pitchers, seen here arranged on a table—are used for octopus fishing (bottom).

delicious marzipans are made in every color imaginable and molded into appetizing little sculptures in the shape of fruit and vegetables. There are other marvels too—such as the *morgado* (*majorat* administrator) and the *dom Rodrigo,* which owe their aristocratic names to the refinement of their preparation and packaging. Almond paste, egg yolks, pumpkin jam, and sugar decoration make these sweets irresistible.

To accompany such desserts the lady of the house offers a wide variety of sweet wines, brandies, and moscatels, liqueurs whose recipes she guards jealously. A glass of *medronheira velha,* an old arbutus brandy, savored on an Algarve terrace at nightfall, brings on an incomparably good mood.

THE SEAMARK, A BEAUTIFUL BELVEDERE. Unlike Christina von Rosen, who has settled inland, António and Bénédicte Fragoso have chosen to live by the sea, on the Sotavento coast where some of the most handsome houses in the Algarve are found. They moved into the Quinta da Barra on the heights of Tavira nearly ten years ago. Since then the couple has been unable to leave this former seventeenth-century manor house that was once the residence of a high-ranking cleric. Because of its prominent location, it once served as a landmark for sailors and one never tires of the fabulous view.

This large house is typical of the region, with elegant ornamented chimneys standing over scissors-truss roofs protected by age-old tiles.

Bénédicte Fragoso has enjoyed herself in creating within this space a harmony of colors: yellow on the walls, gold for baskets filled with fruit, and ochre ceramics. The red of the place mats acts as a counterpoint, while glasses and candlesticks have a gleam of their own.

Windows in the Moorish fashion add yet another touch of exoticism to brilliant white walls. In the heat of summer, the terrace, shaded by a flourishing pink bougainvillaea, is an inviting spot. Here the early mornings are cool and the nights gentle. Time appears to stand still.

Bénédicte and António have skillfully taken this history-laden house in hand, emphasizing its fine whitewashed brick vaulting, the wide wooden laths of its ceilings and the superb *ladrilhos,* terra-cotta tiles that cover the floors. With her own personal blend of tact and freedom, Bénédicte has breathed something of the Algarve's *joie de vivre* into the house. By painting certain walls she brought life back to layers of paint that had cracked, flaked, been reworked and repainted almost every year for centuries. She speaks respectfully of these coverings, which, over the course of years, from simple coats of lime, have come to constitute the walls' memory.

To add to the charm of this *quinta,* the owners of the house have surrounded themselves with carefully chosen painted furniture, ceramics, and baskets—not to mention paintings, their great passion. Among the works decorating the walls of the living room one finds a painting by Alberto de Hutra, António's grandfather and a friend of Fernando Pessoa. Bénédicte also shows her friends round her gallery in Tavira. There, in an enchanting patrician house by the water, she exhibits a selection of sculptures and contemporary artworks.

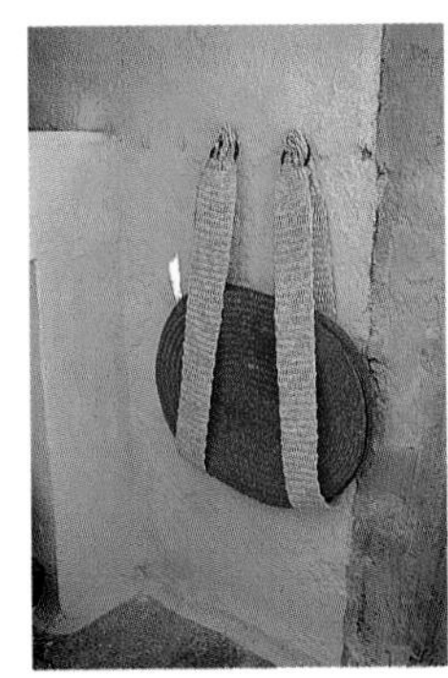

There is a hint of the Orient here, in the house's pointed arches. The white surfaces of the dining room are suffused with the Algarve light (left).

On the terrace, the pink of bougainvillaeas seems to echo that of the wicker furniture (top).

Wood dries in the Algarve sun (bottom).

A canopied bed is covered with a *colcha* of embossed cotton (far right).

A bell to chime the hours. The Portuguese have become masters in ways to appreciate time. The secret of their lifestyle is to enjoy every passing moment to the full. Here we see the Quinta do Vesúvio in the Upper Douro (page 240).

The Portuguese have a talent for enlivening the daily routine. A slave tranquilly scales fish in the kitchen of the Pimenta Palace, which is now Lisbon's city museum (page 241).

Visitor's Guide

These addresses were gathered over the course of many stays in Portugal during which we built friendships with our Portuguese hosts. Some of them are well known; others are finds.
Of course, this guide includes the addresses of all the hotels and restaurants mentioned or illustrated in the preceding chapters, with references to the pages with photographs. We have confined our choice of museums to small, intimate museums of decorative and folk art and to a few palaces that are open to the public. It is impossible for us to mention all of Portugal's many fine hotels, so we have chosen the places that offer the most charm, character and authenticity. We also recommend two very typical forms of Portuguese accommodations, pousadas *and* turismo de habitação *(staying as a guest in a private home), which is especially widespread in the northern part of the country. The accommodations are clearly identified by H (hotel), P (*pousada*) or TH (*turismo de habitação*). Contact the following organizations for general information on* pousadas *and* turismo de habitação*:* **Enatur-Pousadas** *of Portugal, avenida Santa Joana Princesa, 10, Lisbon, Tel: (01) 848 12 21,* **Pitt**, *rua Frederico Arouca, 72, 2°F, Cascais, Tel: (01) 484 44 64,* **Privetur**, *largo das Pereiras, Ponte de Lima, Tel: (058) 7414 93,* **Turihab**, *Praça da República, Ponte de Lima, Tel: (058) 74 16 72 and* **Anter**, *Quinta do Campo, Valado dos Frades, Nazaré, Tel : (062) 57 71 35.*
This guide is organized by region according to the itinerary suggested in the book. The addresses within each region are classified by theme and by alphabetical order of the cities, towns and villages appearing on the maps on pages 245 and 247. We have selected many addresses in the north and in Alentejo for people who enjoy traveling off the beaten track.
The country code for calling telephone numbers in Portugal is 351, which is followed by the local area code. If calling from outside Portugal do not dial the zero, which is used only within the country. Be careful, the telephone numbering system is being changed and the numbers below are likely to be modified.

The provinces of Portugal

MINHO AND DOURO

WHERE TO STAY

Casa de Pascoaes (TH)
Maria Amélia Teixeira de Vasconcellos
São João de Gatão, 4600 Amarante
Tel: (055) 42 25 95
(see pp. 50, 51)
In this region where *vinho verde* has an especially fine reputation, the beautiful eighteenth-century manor house features a wide balcony overlooking the river and hills. Excellent typical cuisine.

Paço da Glória (TH)
Maurício Macedo e Moreira
Jolda, 4970 Arcos de Valdevez
Tel: (058) 94 71 77
(see p. 46)
Artfully restored by the present owner, this manor in the style of English country houses has always been a favorite of artists. One of its magical charms is breakfast served on the poetic arcaded upper gallery overlooking the river Lima.

Quinta de Santa Comba (TH)
Jorge Henrique Carvalho de Campos
Lugar de Crujaes, 4750 Barcelos
Tel: (053) 83 21 01
(see p. 49)
In the heart of a *vinho verde* vineyard, the impressive baroque portal along with the chapel make this a prestigious residence. The warm, friendly manor house opens out onto a flower-bedecked patio. Riders will enjoy the estate's horses.

Casa do Campo (TH)
Maria Armanda de Meireles
Molares, 4890 Celorico de Basto
Tel: (055) 36 12 31
(see pp. 48, 49)
This stately mansion, which welcomes guests from all over the world, exemplifies an artful lifestyle. The austerity of the granite contrasts with the whiteness of the walls. The garden, one of the area's most beautiful, features porticoes and huge bowers of topiary camellias.

Casa do Ribeiro (TH)
Maria do Carmo Ferraz Pinto
São Cristovão de Selho, 4800 Guimarães
Tel: (053) 53 28 81
Guests at this country house walk through a portal crowned by a coat of arms. The antique furniture, silverware, portraits, and chapel give it the charm of a family home. Delightful garden.

Casa de Sezim (TH)
António et Maria Francisca Pinto Mesquita
Nespereira, Apartado 410, 4800 Guimarães
Tel: (053) 52 31 96
(see pp. 40, 41, 42, 43)
This wonderful seignorial house has a few elegant, cosy rooms overlooking the garden. One of the area's most beautiful country homes.

Paço de São Cipriano (TH)
João et Maria Teresa de Sottomayor
Tabuadelo, 4800 Guimarães
Tel: (053) 48 13 37
(see p. 47)
A chapel, crenelated tower, library, patio, and granite kitchen make this ancient palace a place of great character. The residence is surrounded by beautiful gardens with sculpted boxwood, orchards, and vineyards.

Pousada de Santa Marinha (P)
4800 Guimarães
Tel: (053) 51 44 53
This splendid baroque monastery, restored by the renowned architect Fernando Távora, is a warm, friendly place to stay. The huge vaulted corridor leads to the former monks' cells, which have been turned into bedrooms. A delicious *arroz de cabrito*—venison with rice—is served in the spacious arcaded dining room.

Casa de Rodas (TH)
Maria Luisa Tavora
Lugar de Rodas, 4950 Moncão
Tel: (051) 65 21 05
Located on an estate producing *vinho verde*, this residence's frescoes, family furniture, and an enclosed boxwood garden immerse guests in the atmosphere of Minho. The kitchen where breakfast is served still has the original granite fireplace and bread oven.

Casa de Casal de Loivos (TH)
Manuel Bernardo de Sampaio Pimentel Pereira Leitão
Casal de Loivos, 5085 Pinhão
Tel: (054) 7 21 49
This seventeenth-century manor offers a sweeping view of the Upper Douro valley. It is a delightful place to stay for those who would like to explore the nearby prestigious port wine estates.

Casa do Outeiro (TH)
João Gomes de Abreu de Lima
Lugar do Outeiro,
4990 Ponte de Lima
Tel: (058) 94 12 06
The manor's owners help keep local traditions alive and gladly offer regional information to their guests. In this land where granite reigns, the house features a fine emblazoned portal, a colonnaded portico, and a vast kitchen.

Paço de Calheiros (TH)
Count of Calheiros
Calheiros, 4990 Ponte de Lima
Tel: (058) 94 71 64
(see pp. 14, 15, 21, 44)
The count of Calheiros was one of the first local homeowners to welcome guests into his residence and many prominent Portuguese figures enjoy staying at his palace. The towers, monumental staircase, chapel, and upper gallery overlooking the Lima valley and mountains are magnificent.

Casa de Requeixo (TH)
Maria Henriqueta Norton
Frades, 4830 Póvoa de Lanhoso
Tel: (053) 63 11 12
This beautifully restored

farmhouse is located between the ancient town of Braga and Peneda-Gerês National Park and across from the manor where the owners live. The bedrooms are typical of a Portuguese family home with eighteenth-century beds made of Brazilian wood and *colchas*, bedspreads that once were part of a bridal trousseau.

Casa do Ameal (TH)
Maria Elisa Faria de Araújo
Rua do Ameal, 119, Meadela, 4900 Viana do Castelo
Tel: (058) 82 24 03
(see p. 45)
All the charm of a typical Portuguese residence can be found in this manor house where a fine costume collection recalls the splendors of yesteryear. This is an ideal place to stay during the mid-August festival of Our Lady of the Agony that takes place in nearby Viano do Castelo. Guest rooms are located in a separate building.

Casa da Boa Viagím (TH)
José et Júlia Teixeira de Queiroz
Areosa, 4900 Viana do Castelo
Tel: (058) 83 58 35
(see p. 49)
Gardens slope down a verdant hill overlooking the sea and water babbles in a lovely fountain. The manor's outbuildings have been turned into very cosy accommodations.

Quinta do Paço d'Anha (TH)
Antonio Julio et Maria Augusta d'Alpuim
Vila Nova de Anha, 4900 Viana do Castelo
Tel: (058) 32 24 59
(see p. 46)
This historic manor's outbuildings have been converted into comfortable apartments that open out onto the patio. Be sure to sample the outstanding Paço d'Anha *vihno verde* produced on the property.

RESTAURANTS

Arantes
Avenida da Liberdade, 33, 4750 Barcelos
Tel: (053) 81 16 45
The novelist José Saramago immortalized one of this restaurant's specialties, *papas de sarabulho*, a hearty soup made of pork, tripe, and blood, which is served only in winter. During the summer the chef offers *pade de anho*, leg of lamb roasted over a wood fire.

Encanada
Avenida Marginal, 4990 Ponte de Lima
Tel: (058) 94 11 89
This popular restaurant in the covered market has a view of the bridge and the market stalls. The chef prepares local country fare, including *rojoes a moda do Minho*, pork with tripe, blood, and chestnuts.

PASTRY SHOPS

Confeitaria Salvação
Rua Antonio Barroso, 127, 4750 Barcelos
Tel: (053) 81 13 05
Founded more than one hundred and fifty years ago this pastry shop is considered the finest in Minho. The sweet delights include *laranjas de doce*, candied oranges filled with pumpkin jam, and *belas queijadinhas*, stunning, star-shaped cakes made of cheese, almonds, eggs, and fruit.

Pastelaria Zé Nátario
Rua dos Combatentes da Grande Guerra, 4900 Viana do Castelo
Tel: (058) 82 21 17
This renowned café serves *cafézinho*—a small coffee—with *manjericos de Viana* or *princesas do Lima*, traditional pastries from Upper Minho made with eggs and almonds.

MARKETS

Barcelos
(see p. 22)
Portugal's biggest market is held every Thursday on the campo da República. Poultry, fruit, vegetables, cotton and linen bedspreads, lace, embroidered tablecloths, baskets, and wickerwork, wooden folk toys, crockery and quaint ceramic figurines are on sale.

Ponte de Lima
This small city has preserved Minho's festive traditions, one of them being the market held here every other Monday. Local products as well as a thousand everyday items for country life can be found here, including faïence tableware and Minho household linen.

MUSEUM

Casa de Mateus
5000 Vila Real
Tel: (059) 2 31 21
(see p. 37)
The Casa de Mateus, known worldwide as the Solar de Mateus, is one of Portugal's most beautiful baroque palaces. The splendid park features a boxwood garden and an astonishing cypress-covered avenue. The interior is also open to visitors. Here family furniture and the extensive library have helped to preserve all the glow and charm of a lived-in home. The palace also houses a foundation that organizes many cultural activities.

OPORTO

WHERE TO STAY

Casa do Marechal (H)
Avenida da Boavista, 2652
Tel: (02) 610 47 02
(see p. 68)
This Art Deco villa in the Boavista neighborhood is one of Oporto's most charming hotels. It has recently undergone a tasteful redecoration. Neighborhood business people often lunch in the restaurant.

Hotel Boa-Vista (H)
Esplanada do Castelo, 58, Foz do Douro
Tel: (02) 618 31 75
This comfortable mansion near the mouth of the river Douro in Foz do Douro has been converted into a hotel. The view from the restaurant reminds guests that Oporto is also a summer resort. Ask for a room with a sea view.

Hotel da Bolsa (H)
Rua Ferreira Borges, 101
Tel: (02) 202 67 68
The lovely hotel occupies an old downtown building next to the famous stock exchange. Most rooms have a view of the Douro and the port wine lodges of Vila Nova de Gaia.

Hotel Infante de Sagres (H)
Praça D. Filipa de Lencastre, 62
Tel: (02) 200 81 01
Although this hotel was built in the early fifties, it glows with the atmosphere of an old Portuguese residence. The president of Portugal and members of the English and Spanish royal families stay here. Reception rooms with their oriental carpets, inlaid furniture, Gobelins tapestries, Chinese porcelain, and beautiful antiques are superb. Some of the antiques are from the distinguished Casa de Serralves, which belonged to the hotel's owner.

Hotel Internacional (H)
Rua do Almada, 131
Tel: (02) 200 50 32
An oasis of peace and quiet in the heart of town, this small hotel's beautiful staircase and stone arcades attest to the building's monastic past. The hotel houses the famous O Almada restaurant, which is crowded at lunchtime.

RESTAURANTS

Aleixo
Rua da Estação, 216
Tel: (02) 57 04 62
Aleixo is an Oporto institution that serves authentic Portuguese family cooking. Prominent figures such as the writer José Saramago enjoy gathering here.

Boa Nova
Leça da Palmeira, 4450 Matozinhos
Tel: (02) 995 17 85
This seaside restaurant was designed by the architect Alvaro Siza Vieira. It is an enchanting spot to enjoy a glass of port and watch the sun sink into the ocean. The food is excellent.

Mercearia
Cais da Ribeira, 32/33 A
Tel: (02) 200 43 89
(See p. 66)
Delicious riverside dining in a warm setting.

O Escondidinho
Rua Passos Manuel, 144
Tel: (02) 200 10 79
This traditional restaurant has always been a reference in Oporto.

Portofino
Rua do Padrão, 103, 4100 Foz do Douro
Tel: (02) 617 73 39
The façade's yellow and white geometric azulejos hint at the fine decoration inside. This Foz do Douro restaurant serves very fine cuisine.

Portucale
Rua da Alegria, 598
Tel: (02) 57 07 17
The large twelfth-floor dining room has a sweeping view of Oporto and the sea. The restaurant, considered one of the city's finest, is a must for anyone who wants to enjoy great Portuguese cuisine and regional specialties.

Taverna do Bebodos
Cais da Ribeira, 21/25
Tel: (02) 31 35 65
(see p. 62)
This waterfront tavern is a well-known address in Portugal. For over a hundred years, guests in the vaulted dining room have been enjoying northern specialties such as *papas de sarabulho*, a soup made famous by José Saramago.

WINES

The Vila Nova de Gaia wine lodges
(see p. 70)
The names of the nearly 80 companies that do business here are spelled out in gigantic rooftop letters. Some of the lodges are over two hundred years old.
Oak casks and huge tuns are stacked beneath dark, vaulted ceilings. After a tour visitors can taste and purchase port.

The best-known houses include:
Ferreira, Rua da Carvalhosa, 19/103
Tel: (02) 370 00 10
(see p. 72)
Ramos-Pinto, Avenida Ramos-Pinto, 380
Tel: (02) 30 07 16
(see p. 70, 71, 72)
Taylor's, Rua do Choupelo, 250 Tel: (02) 371 99 99
(see p. 71)
W & J Graham & Co, Quinta do Agro, Rua Rei Ramiro
Tel: (02) 379 60 63

Aside from the Vila Nova de Gaia lodges, fine ports can be found in special shops called *garrafeiras*. We recommend the following two:

Garrafeira do Campo Alegre
Rua do Campo Alegre, 1598
Tel: (02) 618 82 95
Garrafeira Augusto Leite
Rua do Passeio Alegre, 924
Tel: (02) 618 34 24

To taste port the right way:
Solar do Vinho do Porto
Quinta da Macieirinha, rua de Entre-Quintas, 220
Tel: (02) 69 77 93
In a downtown park just below the charming Romantic museum, this bar and small garden overlook the Douro.
Experts from the Oporto Wine Institute, called *escancoes*, introduce visitors to the subtleties of port. Over 250 wines from sixty or so firms can be tasted.

PASTRY SHOPS

Casa Margaridense
Travessa de Cedofeita 20-A
Tel: (02) 200 11 78
(see p. 64, 65)
This renowned pastry shop features tasty traditional sweets such as *marmelada*, made from quince paste, and *pão de ló,* a soft, moist sponge cake shaped like a wheel.

Confeitaria Império
Rua Santa Catarina 149/151
Tel: (02) 200 55 95
(see p. 65)
One of the city's oldest and finest pastry shops.

FOOD STORES

A Pérola da Guiné
Rua Costa Cabral, 231
Tel: (02) 52 02 28
(see p. 65)
As the azulejos suggest, this grocery store specializes in coffee from Portugal's former colonies, especially Brazil.

A Pérola do Bolhão
Rua Formosa 279
Tel: (02) 200 40 09
(see p. 63)
Tea, coffee, dried fruit, port, and specialties from Brazil are on display behind a well-known, entertaining façade.

Casa Oriental
Campo Martires da Pátria, 112
Tel: (02) 200 25 30
(see p. 62)
Cod is king here. Stacked to the tops of the windows, it is sold from a metal-clad counter. A wide range of origins and quality make choosing an art in itself.

BOOKSTORE

Lello & Irmão
Rua dos Carmelitas, 144
Tel: (02) 200 20 37
(see p. 67)
This bookstore features amazing neo-Gothic architecture and carved woodwork. Lello & Irmão have published the greatest nineteenth-century Portuguese writers, including Eça de Queiroz and Camilo Castelo Branco.

BOUTIQUES

Luís Ferreira & Filhos
Rua Trindade Coelho, 9
Tel: (02) 31 61 46
Luís Ferreira is regarded as Oporto's best goldsmith, and some people think he is the finest in the country. An absolutely enchanting boutique.

José Rosas
Rua Eugénio de Castro, 282
Tel: (02) 69 57 85
Northern Portugal's most prominent families have been coming to this goldsmith for more than one hundred and fifty years.

Miguel Vaz de Almada
Rua Delfim Ferreira, 500
Tel: (02) 610 44 72
This young jeweler's prices are highly competitive.

MARKETS

Bolhão Market
Rua Sa da Bandeira
(see pp. 53, 54, 60, 61)
In central Oporto the Bolhão covered market features a superb iron structure. This is the best place to discover the north's fine food specialties, including sausage, poultry, fish, and all kinds of beans on display in beautiful, cloth-draped baskets.

Ribeira Market
(see p. 62)
This picturesque outdoor market is held on the Ribeira waterfront. Boats plying the Douro supplied it until just a few years ago.

MUSEUM

Casa de Serralves
Rua de Serralves, 977
Tel: (02) 617 51 24
(see pp. 68, 69)
The Casa de Serralves is a lavish, 1930s villa surrounded by Art Deco gardens and a huge park. It is open to the public and houses a cultural foundation that will become the museum of contemporary art. The small tea room with its fragrant wisteria plants is a delightful spot to relax in the park.

ON THE ROAD SOUTH

WHERE TO STAY

Cúria Palace Hotel (H)
Cúria 3780 Anadia
Tel: (031) 51 21 31
(see p. 108, 109)
Built to resemble a huge ocean liner, the vast lobbies and dining rooms of this 1920s grand hotel bring to mind those of a cruise ship. The pool, set in the middle of a vineyard, was once one of Europe's largest. A nostalgic throwback to the luxurious ocean crossings of yesterday.

Paloma Branca (H)
Rua Luís Gomes de Carvalho, 23
3800 Aveiro
Tel: (034) 2 25 29
This hotel occupies an elegant 1930s mansion. The furniture, *objets d'art*, and delightful garden with fountain give it the feel of a charming private residence.

Hotel Pálacio de Águeda (H)
Quinta da Borralha, 3750 Agueda (near Aveiro)
Tel: (034) 60 19 77
Jean Louis de Talancé has turned the count da Borralha's lavish residence, located between Oporto and Lisbon, into a cheerful, elegant hotel. Furniture, *objets d'art*, and fabrics blend in perfectly with the late-eighteenth-century setting. A warm welcome, a renowned restaurant, and a garden add to the charm.

Paço da Ermida (TH)
João Alberto Ferreira Pinto Basto
3830 Ilhavo (near Aveiro)
Tel: (034) 32 24 96
This residence is owned by the family of the founder of the Vista Alegre porcelain workshop and museum. Guests walk up a beautiful double flight of steps to enter the elegant nineteenth-century palace.

Pousada da Ria (P)
Torreira, 3870 Murtosa (near Aveiro)
Tel: (034) 4 83 32
A journey to the end of the earth. The *pousada*, located on a strip of land between the sea and the *ria*, has fine views of the lagoon, the sea, and the sky. Don't leave without tasting the house specialty, *ensopado de enguias*—eels stewed in wine sauce.

Buçaco Palace Hotel (H)
Buçaco, 3050 Mealhada
Tel: (031) 93 01 01
(see pp. 77, 110, 111, 112, 113)
This beautiful turn-of-the-century Manueline palace in the heart of a wonderful forest is regarded as one of Europe's finest hotels. Meals in the rotunda opening out on the park are moments of grace. The wine cellar is particularly renowned.

Hotel Astória (H)
Avenida Emídio Navarro, 21, 3000 Coimbra
Tel: (039) 2 20 55
On the banks of the river Mondego in the heart of town, the hotel radiates all the charm of a 1930s residence. Portuguese painters and writers once enjoyed staying here. Amália Rodrigues sang her fantastic fados in the hotel. The restaurant offers very rare vintages from Buçaco.

Quinta de Santa Bárbara (TH)
Manuel Vieira de Faria
2250 Constância
Tel: (049) 9 92 14
(see p. 107)
This hotel glows with the warm atmosphere of a traditional Portuguese home. The former cellar has been converted into an outstanding restaurant specializing in *sopa de peixes*, fish soup from the Ribatejo.

Estalagém do Convento (H)
Rua D. João d'Ornelas, 2510 Óbidos
Tel: (062) 95 92 17
A flower-bedecked patio, stone arcades, wooden ceilings, elegant furniture and a friendly restaurant make this former monastery a charming hotel. Some rooms have a wonderful view of town.

Pousada do Castelo (H)
2510 Óbidos
Tel: (062) 95 91 05
(see p. 107)
While bedrooms in this carefully restored fortress are simple, the dining room and Gothic window corners are elaborate.

Quinta da Sobreira (TH)
Maria João Trigueiro de Mártel Franco Frazão
Vale de Figueira, 2000

Santarém
Tel: (043) 42 02 21
(see pp. 106, 107)
Enjoy the simple pleasures of country life in this comfortable nineteenth-century house.

Quinta de Santo André (H)
Estrada Monte Gordo, 2600
Vila Franca de Xira
Tel: (063) 2 21 43
The rider-owned resort is a delightful spot for a stay in horse country. At Vila de Franca Xira, horseback riding enthusiasts can take prized *haute école* lessons at the Lezíria riding academy, tel: (063) 2 27 81.

RESTAURANTS

Marquês de Marialva
Largo do Romal, 3060
Cantanhede
Tel: (031) 42 00 10
Marquês de Marialva is widely regarded as one of the area's finest restaurants. The *chanfana de cabra*—marinaded venison—and the *leitão assado*—suckling pig on a spit—are two very tasty local specialties.

Restaurante Ramalhão
Rua Tenente Valadim, 24,
3140 Montemor-o-Velho
(near Cantanhede)
Tel: (039) 6 84 35
This highly regarded restaurant features authentic local cuisine in a rustic setting. The *bacalhau com migas temperado com ervas aromáticas*, a dish of cod made with bread and a blend of aromatic herbs, is a must. Chosen by the Michelin guide.

A Ilustre Casa de Ramiro
Rua Porta do Vale, 2510
Óbidos
Tel: (062) 95 91 94
White columns punctuate the beautiful vaulted dining room painted in red. Huge terra-cotta jars from Porto de Mós stand against the walls and highlight a setting designed by the architect José Fernandes Teixeira. Flavorful meats are roasted in an imposing fireplace flanked by granite pillars.

CAFÉS AND BARS

Café Santa Cruz
Praça 8 de Maio,
3000 Coimbra
Tel: (039) 3 36 17
The vaulted chapel of Santa Cruz church has been converted into a spectacular café popular with students.

Ibn Errik Rex
Rua Direita, 2510 Óbidos
Tel: (062) 9 51 93
This offbeat bar with frescoes is the most popular spot to meet in Óbidos. *Ginjinha*, a famous liqueur made with the region's cherries, is a house specialty.

PASTRY SHOP

Café Zaira
Praça da República, 18,
2500 Caldas da Rainha
Tel: (062) 83 22 88
Cavacas, a sweet treat similar to macaroons, and *trouxas de ovos*, croquettes made of sugar and eggs, are two of the excellent pastries served at this market square café.

CERAMICS

Loja da Vista Alegre
Vista Alegre, 3830 Ilhavo
(near Aveiro)
Tel: (034) 32 42 23
Superb, attractively priced seconds can be found in this shop near the Vista Alegre porcelain factory.

Rafael Bordalo Pinheiro
Rua Rafael Bordalo Pinheiro,
53, 2500 Caldas da Rainha
Tel: (062) 84 23 53
Seconds shop of the most famous factory in Caldas da Rainha, the faïence capital.

Secla
Rua São João de Deus, 37,
2500 Caldas da Rainha
Tel: (062) 84 21 51
This shop also has a wide

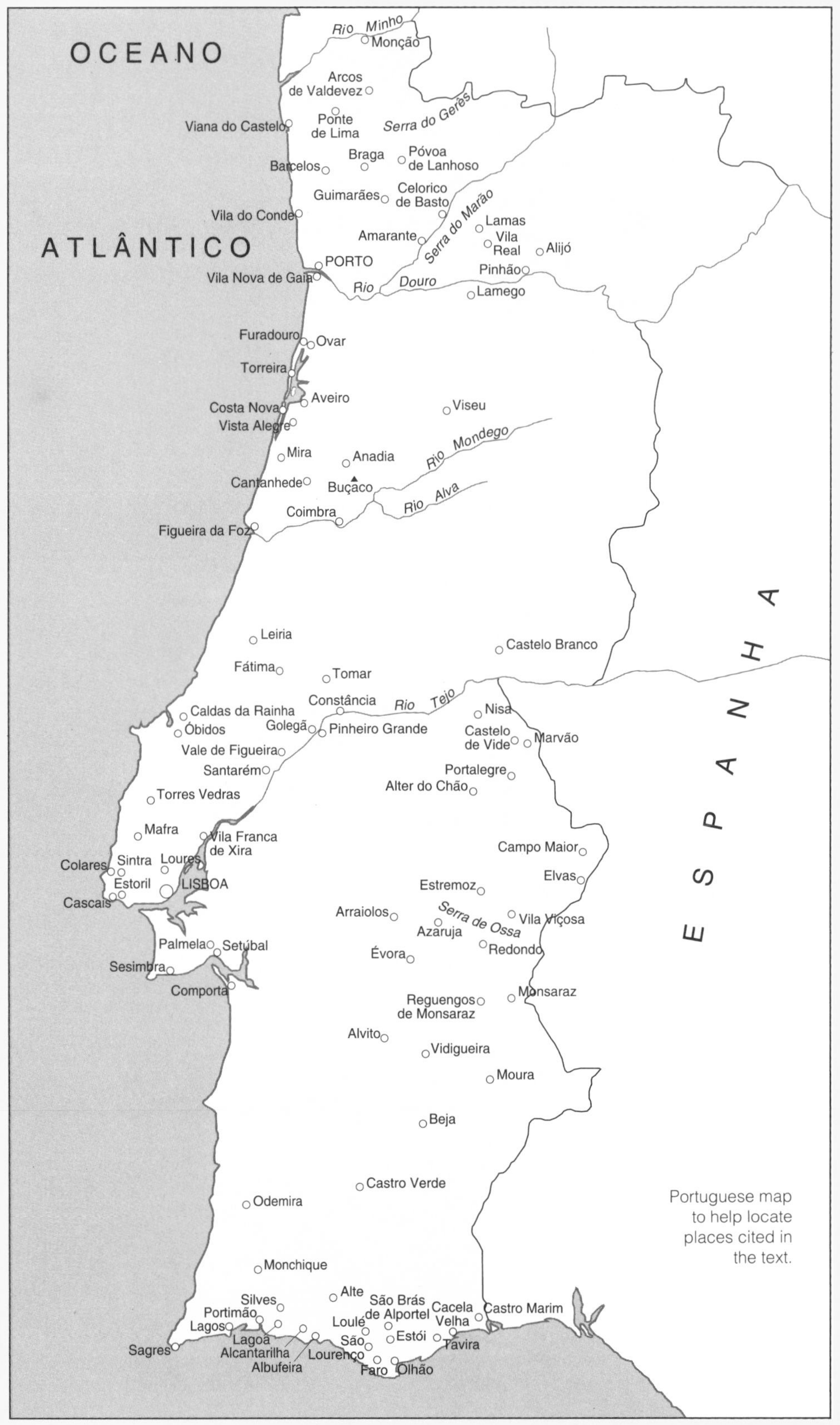

Portuguese map to help locate places cited in the text.

range of faïence, but the styles are less traditional.

MARKET

Coimbra
(see p. 88)
The market is held every day except Sunday on the rua Olimpo Nicolau Rui Fernandes overlooking the city. Everything can be found here, from local farm produce to fish from the nearby port of Figueira da Foz, clothes, and everyday items like locally crafted baskets.

MUSEUMS

Vista Alegre Historical Museum
Vista Alegre, 3830 Ilhavo (near Aveiro)
Tel: (034) 32 50 40
The museum is owned by the same family that founded the Vista Alegre workshop, Portugal's most renowned maker of porcelain. Beautiful masterpieces designed by the distinguished house since 1824 are on display.

Rafael Bordalo Pinheiro Museum
Rua Rafael Bordalo Pinheiro, 53, 2500 Caldas da Rainha
Tel: (062) 84 23 53
Ceramic lovers should not pass up the opportunity to visit this small museum, within the famous Caldas da Rainha workshop founded by Rafael Bordalo Pinheiro in the nineteenth century.

AROUND LISBON

WHERE TO STAY

Casa da Pérgola (TH)
Manuel Correa Gonçalves
Avenida Valbom, 13,
2750 Cascais
Tel: (01) 284 00 40
A lovely garden surrounds this cosy nineteenth-century family home in the heart of town. The façade features magnificent azulejo window frames.

Pousada de Palmela (P)
2950 Palmela
Tel: (01) 235 12 26
This fifteenth-century monastery overlooks the imposing Serra da Arrábida. The magnificently restored buildings are of a size that is far from austere. The rooms, especially numbers 9 and 22, have spectacular views.

Pousada de São Filipe (P)
2900 Setúbal
Tel: (065) 52 38 44
(see p. 142)
Rooms with a view are wonderful in this *pousada* that occupies a citadel overlooking the town and the river. Mealtimes on the terrace are an enchanting moment. The menu features fish and shellfish from the Setúbal region.

Quinta das Torres (H)
Vila Nogueira de Azeitão,
2900 Setúbal
Tel: (01) 218 00 01
(see p. 139)
Life in this beautiful Renaissance manor is sweet. The rooms are warm and elegant; one of them is in the tower. The dining room, which is graced with azulejo panels and rare Italian majolicas, looks out onto a charming ornamental pool.

Seteais Palace Hotel (H)
Rua Barbosa do Bocage, 8,
2710 Sintra
Tel: (01) 923 32 00
(see pp. 140, 141)
Every moment of a stay in this splendid historic residence is a delight. The neoclassical Portuguese furniture in the salons and bedrooms is very elegant. The gardens and their lovely sculpted boxwood are worthy of a palace. An outstanding restaurant features local specialties, especially *pescada*—hake from Cabo da Roca—and *frango estufado*—coq au vin Colares style.

Quinta da Capela (TH)
Arturo da Silva Pereira
Estrada de Monserrate,
2710 Sintra.
Tel: (01) 929 01 70
(see pp. 116, 138)
A great amount of care and effort has clearly gone into furnishing this typical Portuguese home. The harmoniously-scaled residence is on an outstanding site near the Monserrate gardens. Accommodations are available in two other charming houses on the property as well.

Quinta de São Thiago (TH)
Maria Teresa Braddell
Estrada de Monserrate,
2710 Sintra.
Tel: (01) 923 29 23
This *quinta* sums up all of Sintra's charms with a breathtaking view, trees that are hundreds of years old and a Renaissance manor. The welcome is warm and friendly and the food served in the azulejo-decorated dining room is excellent.

QUINTAS AND PALACES FOR RENT

Quinta de Manique
Marquis and Marchioness of Casteja
Alcabideche, 2750 Cascais
(see pp. 124, 125, 134, 135)
For rental accommodations:
Sociedade Campos Henriques (CH) Tel: (01) 396 70 51
The wonderful pink stucco residence is decorated with azulejos. The lounges have family furniture, water babbles in the shady gardens, and a huge tent in the park can be rented for distinguished receptions year round except in July and August.

Correio-Mor Palace
2670 Loures
Tel: (1) 983 33 31
(see p. 121)
For rental accommodations:
Sociedade Imobiliária e Turística, Rua Rodrigo da Fonseca, 53-2°, 1200 Lisboa
Tel: (01) 386 34 13
One of the most lavish dwellings in the Lisbon area, this palace was built in the eighteenth century when gold was flowing in from Brazil. Both the palace and gardens can be rented for receptions. Visits are also possible by appointment.

Quinta da Bacalhoa
Vila Fresca de Azeitão,
2900 Setúbal
Tel: (01) 218 00 11
(see pp. 130, 131, 132, 133)
For rental accommodations:
Thomas W. Scoville,
3637 Veazey Street, N.W.,
Washington D.C., 20008, USA.
Tel: (1) 202-686-7336
The palace and gardens are considered masterpieces of the Portuguese Renaissance. They are owned by an American family in love with Portugal. Living in this outstanding setting is a unique experience, but reservations must be made well in advance.

RESTAURANTS

Porto de Santa Maria
Praia do Guincho, 2750 Cascais
Tel: (01) 285 04 91
Poised between sky and sea, this seafood restaurant is the best in the area. The *arroz de mariscos*—rice with seafood—is wonderful. Stars in the Michelin guide.

Cozinha Velha, Palácio Nacional de Queluz
Largo do Palácio, 2745 Queluz (near Lisbon)
Tel: (01) 435 02 32
This restaurant is in what was once the royal palace's huge kitchen. It features an enormous fireplace supported by eight columns, gleaming copperware, and excellent desserts displayed on a beautiful marble table. Visitors to the royal palace can also drop in here for a refreshment.

WINES

J.M. da Fonseca Internacional Vinhos Lda.
Vila Nogueira de Azeitão,
2925 Azeitão (near Setúbal)
Tel: (01) 218 02 27
This is the Lancers Rosé and Mateus Rosé winery, and the outstanding wines produced by the João Pires Vinhos company headed by António Francisco Avillez are aged in the lodges here. Mr. Avillez's large antique azulejo collection is also on display. Tours are available.

PASTRY SHOP

Casa Piriquita
Rua das Padarias, 1/3,
Sintra
Tel: (01) 923 06 26
Sintra's finest pastry shop is on a tiny street near the royal palace. The *queijadas*, fresh cheese tarts with sugar, are legendary here.

AZULEJOS

São Simão Arte
Rua Almirante Reis, 86,
Vila Fresca de Azeitão, 2925 Azeitão (near Setúbal)
Tel: (01) 218 31 35
This workshop designs azulejos and creates entire panels according to traditional methods. Visitors can make purchases at the workshop or place orders.

FAIR

Arts and Crafts Fair
Junta de Turismo, Arcadas do Parque, 2765 Estoril
Tel: (01) 468 01 13
Artisans from all over Portugal come here to display their works in July and August. Sometimes this is the only place you can find *bonecos*—figurines from Estremoz—and azulejos painted by hand in small, specialized workshops.

MUSEUM

Fronteira Palace
Fundacão das Casas de Fronteira e Alorna
Largo São Domingos, 1,
Benfica, 1500 Lisbon
Tel: (01) 778 20 23
(see pp. 136, 137)
The Fronteira Palace and its extraordinary gardens on the

edge of Lisbon are open to the public. The azulejos here are gorgeous. They cover terraces, pools, and fountains as well as the inside of the magnificently decorated palace, which is still lived in by the owners.

LISBON

WHERE TO STAY

Albergaria Senhora do Monte
Calçada do Monte, 39 (H)
Tel: (1) 886 60 02
From the heights overlooking Lisbon, this hotel has a beautiful view of Saint George's Castle, but it can be very difficult to find.

As Janelas Verdes (H)
Rua das Janelas Verdes, 47
Tel: (01) 396 81 43
Some rooms in this elegantly decorated hotel enjoy a view of the harbor. The late-eighteenth-century residence is especially prized in the summer months when guests can have breakfast or enjoy a glass of madeira on the ivy-covered patio.

Avenida Palace (H)
Rua Primeiro de Dezembro, 123
Tel: (01) 346 01 51
This recently restored, turn-of-the-century hotel is on one of the city's busiest squares. The Avenida Palace boasts one of the city's most famous interiors. The inlaid furniture, marble sculpture, bronze statues, mirrors, Arraiolos carpets, and glass lamps give visitors the pleasant feeling of being hotel regulars.

Lisboa Plaza (H)
Avenida da Liberdade/
Travessa do Salitre
Tel: (01) 346 39 22
Nestled in the heart of Lisbon, this very elegant hotel has the charm of a warm, friendly home. Graça Viterbo has designed the interior decoration—from the light-toned imitation marble, to the porcelain and the prints on the wall—in a very classical spirit.

Veneza Lisboa (H)
Avenida da Liberdade, 189
Tel: (01) 352 67 00
This beautiful, entirely renovated, and well-located nineteenth-century residence is a wonderful hotel.

York House (H)
Rua das Janelas Verdes, 32
Tel: (01) 396 24 35
(see p. 173)
Near the beautiful Abrantes Palace, which houses the French embassy, this former monastery is the most poetic hotel in Lisbon and as elegant as any Portuguese palace. It is furnished with canopy beds and decorated with azulejos and Arraiolos carpets. The city's hustle and bustle is swiftly forgotten during a meal accompanied by singing birds in the wonderful indoor garden .

RESTAURANTS

A Bota Alta
Travessa da Queimada, 37
Tel: (01) 342 79 59
Drawings and autographs of celebrities who have been to this Bairro Alto restaurant cover the walls. The atmosphere is fun and cosmopolitan. *Bacalhau à Brás*—cod with eggs—is a house specialty.

Alcãntara Café
Rua Maria Luisa Holstein, 15
Tel: (01) 363 71 76
(see p. 170)
This former warehouse has been turned into a trendy, innovatively decorated restaurant.

António Clara - Clube de Empresário
Avenida da Republica, 38
Tel: (01) 76 63 80
One of Lisbon's best restaurants is housed in this early-twentieth-century palace. The cod is delicious in this gathering spot for Portugal's political and financial elite.

Aviz
Rua Serpa Pinto, 12-B
Tel: (01) 342 83 91
Crystal chandeliers, velvet, and damask decorate this mecca of fine dining in the Chiado neighborhood. Specialties include the *costeletas de porco recheadas com ameijoas*, pork chops stuffed with clams—a superb interpretion of a traditional dish.

Casa da Comida
Travessa das Amoreiras, 1
Tel: (01) 388 53 76
(see p. 172)
Lisbon's trendiest crowd meets at this restaurant. A patio, East India Company china, and paintings create a very Portuguese mood. The delicious food is made with the finest ingredients. Menu highlights include the *faisão à moda do Convento de Alcântara*, pheasant marinaded in port wine and garnished with truffles, a great classic from Estremadura. Stars in the Michelin guide.

Cervejaria da Trindade
Rua Nova da Trindade, 20
Tel: (01) 342 35 06
(see p. 164)
This lively brasserie is a favorite haunt of journalists, writers, and students. Terrific Sagres beer flows freely here.

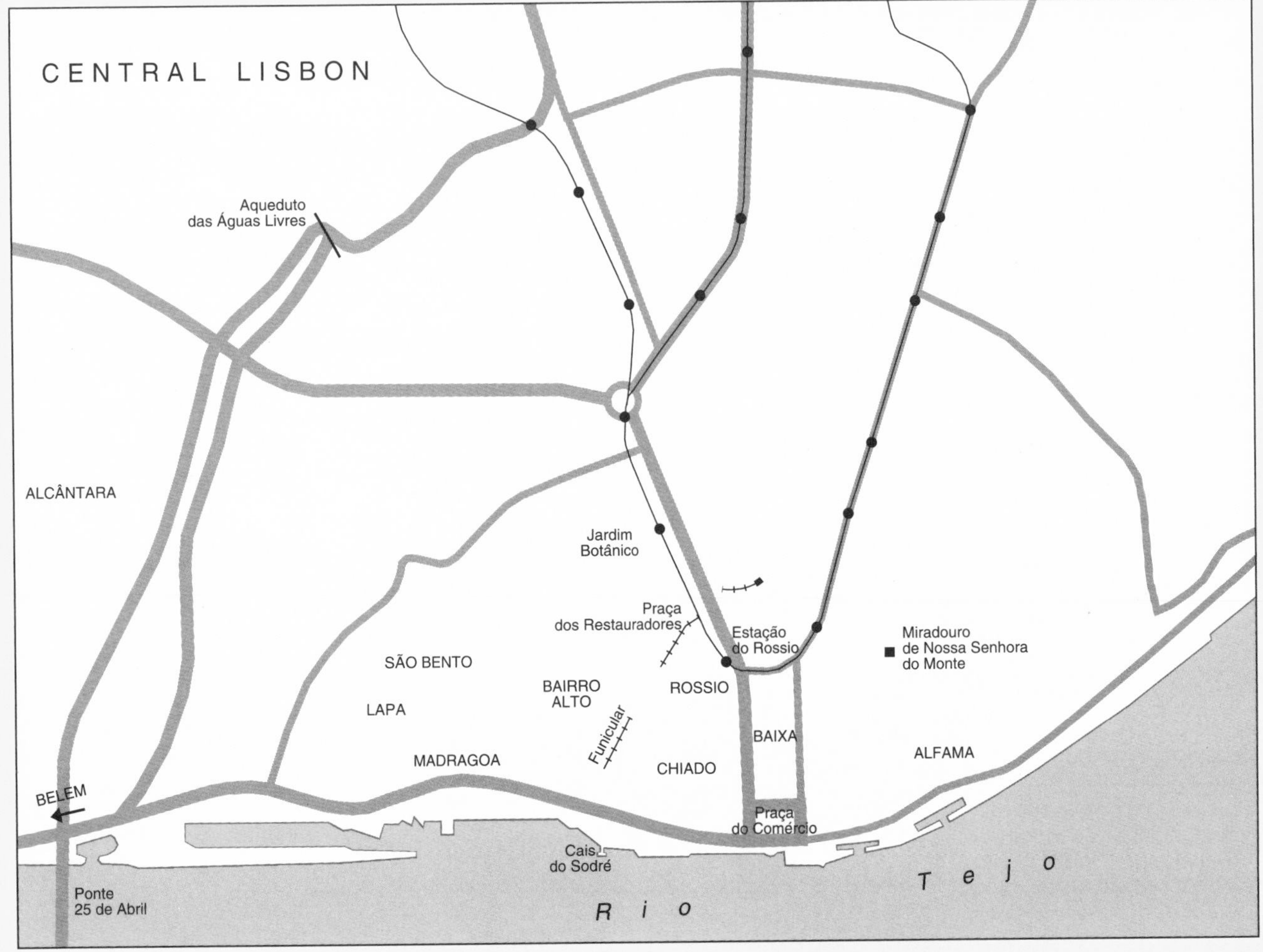

Conventual
Praça das Flores, 45
Tel: (01) 60 91 96
Besides the religious scenes in sculpted wood, the other original touch of this restaurant is the menu, consisting of age-old, mouth-watering dishes prepared in monasteries. Some people think this is the best restaurant in Lisbon. Stars in the Michelin guide.

Gambrinus
Rua das Portas de Santo Antão, 23
Tel: (1) 342 14 66
This restaurant is famous for its fine menu, especially the seafood specialties. The wine cellar is one of the best in the city and the wine waiter, Francisco Gonçalves, enjoys an outstanding reputation. Leading literary and financial personalities gather here.

Pap'Açôrda
Rua da Atalaia, 57
Tel: (01) 346 48 11
Mário Soares is one of many who enjoy the free-wheeling atmosphere at this fashionable restaurant. Specialties include tasty Portuguese *açôrdas*, bread sauces that accompany shellfish, cod, or meat.

Tágide
Largo da Academia Nacional de Belas Artes, 18
Tel: (01) 346 05 70
This restaurant is a real institution. The superb Portuguese cuisine includes *lombos de robalo à portuguesa*—Portuguese-style bass—and *costeletas de borrego à Tãgide*—lamb chops done the house way. The dining room is decorated with azulejos and has a fine view of the Tagus.

Versailles
Avenida da República, 15-A
Tel: (01) 355 53 44
(see p. 166)
The Versailles, a combination café-restaurant, is known for its elegant stuccoes and mirrors. Everything here is good, especially the *arroz de pato*, the rice with baked duck, and the *doces d'ovos*, those typically Portuguese cakes made of eggs and sugar.

CAFÉS AND BARS

Café Brasileira
Rua Garrett, 120
Tel: (01) 346 95 41
This historic landmark was once a famous literary haunt, but it no longer lives up to its reputation. A melancholic bronze Pessoa on the terrace recalls that the great author once came here to write.

A Ginjinha
Travessa de São Domingos, 8
Tel: (01) 84 55 37
(see p. 166)
Customers stand at the bar of this tiny tavern to enjoy a delicious Morello cherry liqueur, one of the country's most popular drinks.

O Chapitô
Rua Costa do Castelo, 7
Tel: (01) 888 22 41
A pleasant atmosphere and a shady terrace overlooking Lisbon and Alfama.

Pavilhão Chinês
Rua D. Pedro V, 89
Tel: (01) 342 47 29
(see p. 169)
This well-known bar has an amazing interior.

Procópio
Alto de São Francisco, 21
Tel: (01) 65 28 51
The atmosphere in this turn-of-the-century style café conjures up images of an eighteenth-century salon. Alice Pinto Coelho, the soul of this bar, welcomes business people, political figures, and journalists.

PASTRY SHOP

Antiga Confeitaria de Belém
Rua de Belém, 84
Tel: (01) 363 74 23
(see pp. 164, 165, 167)
This pastry shop, fragrant with the lovely scent of cinnamon, is famous for its *pastéis de Nata*, secret-recipe custard tarts.

NIGHT CLUBS

Frágil
Rua da Atalaia, 126-8
Tel: (01) 346 95 78
Owner Manuel Reis put the Bairro Alto on the map in 1974. The decoration at the Frágil, a real institution, changes every six months. The crowd is motley and the atmosphere colorful.

Kapital
Avenida 24 de Julho, 68
Tel: (01) 395 59 63
Decorator Maria José Salavisa has designed a fantastic setting where columns, chrome-plated mirrors, and totem poles are somewhat suggestive of surrealist German movie sets. This club is thronged by Lisbon's trendiest night owls.

XXIV de Julho
Avenida 24 de Julho, 116
Tel: (01) 396 09 11
(see pp. 170, 171)
A surprising, highly fashionable night club with terrific decoration.

FADO

Fado is sung in *casas de fado*, restaurants, bars, and bistros in the Bairro Alto, Alfama, Alcântara, and Lapa neighborhoods.

Mascote de Atalaia
Rua Atalaia, 47
Tel: (01) 347 04 80
This old Bairro Alto café is one of the few places where the fado, sung by neighborhood residents, is genuine. The room is so small visitors arriving after 8:00 p.m. have to stand in the street.

Senhor Vinho
Rua do Meio à Lapa, 18
Tel: (01) 397 26 81.
Maria da Fé both owns and sings at this friendly, lively restaurant.

AZULEJOS

Cerâmica Constância
Rua São Domingos à Lapa, 8
Tel: (01) 396 39 51
(see p. 174)
This workshop in the Lapa neighborhood skilfully makes copies of old azulejos and designs new ones.

Galeria Ratton Cerámicas
Rua Academia das Ciênças, 2 C
Tel: (01) 346 09 48
Ana Maria Viegas breathes new life into the great Portuguese tradition by commissioning contemporary ceramic artists to design outstanding azulejos that are either made by hand or mass-produced. She will also contact artists to make azulejos based on individual customers' interior decoration.

Sant'Anna
Rua do Alecrim, 95
Tel: (01) 342 25 37
Sant'Anna azulejos have been part of Portugal's way of life since 1741. This tradition is alive and well with a wide choice of models, including life-size welcoming figures and sculptural pieces.

Solar, Albuquerque e Sousa
Rua D. Pedro V, 68
Tel: (01) 346 55 22
(see p. 174)
The country's most famous dealer in antique azulejos. Wonderful pieces ranging from the sixteenth century to the present day can be found in this Ali Baba's cave. Whole panels are for sale.

Viúva Lamego
Largo do Intendente Pina Manique, 25
Tel: (01) 315 24 01
(see pp. 151, 160, 161)
The beautiful façade is just a hint of what's in store inside. Viúva Lamego makes the azulejos seen in the Lisbon metro as well as copies of old tiles.

ARTS AND CRAFTS

Casa Quintão
Rua Ivens, 30
Tel: (01) 346 58 37
This renowned workshop has been giving good advice to buyers of Arraiolos carpets for more than one hundred years. Shoppers can place special orders in addition to choosing from the many models on display in the store.

Casa Regional da Ilha Verde
Rua Paiva de Andrade, 4
Tel: (01) 342 59 74
This shop specializes in crafts from the Azores, especially blue-toned or polychrome embroidery on a white or ivory background.

Casa de São Vicente
Azinhaga das Viegas, 1, Marvila
Tel: (01) 858 11 59
Custom-made Arraiolos carpets are ordered at this store east of Lisbon. The boutique is well-known for the quality of its old designs and the beautiful colors of its wools.

Galeria Tapeçarias de Portalegre
Rua da Academia das Ciênçias, 2
Tel: (01) 342 14 81
The famous, highly esteemed Portalegre workshop makes tightly woven tapestries. Customers can order works designed by contemporary artists.

Madeira House
Rua Augusta, 131-135
Tel: (01) 342 68 13
One of the most exceptional linen shops in Lisbon, it sells beautiful Madeira tablecloths and charming, rustic models from Viana do Castelo. Fine household linen from the north, made from linen fibers woven on hand looms is also found here.

Principe Real Enchovais
Rua Escola Politécnica, 12-14
Tel: (01) 346 59 45
This address is well known the world over. Crowned heads, prominent figures, and famous families come here to place orders with Maria Christina Castro, who founded the shop thirty years ago. She and her son offer the finest cloth graced with wonderful embroidery of intricate stitches such as Richelieu, as well as difficult-to-find lace from Peniche. Personalized models on request.

MUSEUMS

Ricardo do Espírito Santo Silva Foundation
Largo das Portas do Sol, 2

Tel: (01) 886 21 83
(see p. 174)
All the treasures of eighteenth-century Portugal are on display in this Alfama palace that has become a museum of decorative arts. Furniture, china, silverware, and *objets d'art* can be admired here. Workshops next door do restoration, make copies, and create wonderful new items that are sold the world over.

City Museum
Campo Grande, 245
Tel: (01) 759 16 17
(see p. 241)
This museum, which occupies an eighteenth-century palace, is an ode to azulejos. Chinoiserie, mythological scenes, and scenes of daily life decorate the salons, staircases, and the picturesque kitchen.

National Azulejo Museum
Rua do Madre de Deus, 4
Tel: (01) 814 77 47
Portugal's most beautiful collection of azulejos has been assembled in the Madre de Deus convent, which is famous for its rich gilded woodwork and paintings. The charming restaurant overlooking the gardens is decorated with azulejos of cooking themes. Azulejos can be be purchased in the museum's gift shop.

OFF THE BEATEN TRACK

Companhia Carris de Ferro de Lisboa
Rua Primeiro de Maio, 101
Tel: (01) 363 93 43
Streetcars can be rented here for a private tour of the city. A unique experience.

THE ALENTEJO

WHERE TO STAY

Castelo do Alvito (P)
7920 Alvito
Tel: (084) 4 83 43
This recently restored, impressive-looking fortress is bristling with five towers. Some rooms in the elegant *pousada* still have their Gothic vaulting. One of them is the dining room, where guests can savor the *bacalhau à marquês de Alvito*. The cool gardens are fragrant with the wonderful scent of orange trees.

Convento de São Paulo (H)
Aldeia da Serra, Serra d'Ossa, 7170 Redondo
Tel: (066) 99 91 00
(see p. 210, 211)
This lavish hotel was once a monastery appreciated by members of the royal family over the centuries. Noteworthy details include vaulted ceilings, over one hundred azulejos, and marble fountains babbling with mountain water.

Pousada da Rainha Santa Isabel (P)
7100 Estremoz
Tel: (068) 2 26 18
(see p. 208)
Elegant lounges and rooms graced with old furniture fill this fantastic setting of stone, marble, and woodwork. The huge, vaulted dining room offers fine food. This is hunting country, and a wide choice of game is available in season. A wonderful Borba wine goes well with the *lebre à caçadora*, hunter's style hare.

Quinta do Monte dos Pensamentos (TH)
Cristovão Tomas Bach Andresen Leitão
Estrada da Estacão do Ameixial, 7100 Estremoz
Tel: (068) 2 23 75
(see p. 209)
This welcoming, white-butressed *monte alentejano* was a hunting lodge until just a few years ago. The owners have opened it to the public and today guests can see an amazing collection of ceramics that seem to have taken over the whole house. The coolness under the arbors is quite refreshing during the hot summer months.

O Eborense Solar Monfalim (H)
Largo da Misericodia, 1, 7000 Évora
Tel: (066) 2 20 31
Located in the heart of town, this small Renaissance palace still has a huge marble staircase covered with green plants. The arcaded loggia is a great place for a drink at sunset.

Pousada dos Lóios (P)
Largo Conde Vila Flor, 7000 Évora
Tel: (066) 2 40 51
(see p. 209)
This former monastery decorated with marble, azulejos, and frescoes is one of the most irresistible *pousadas* in the area. The monks' famous sweets are sinfully delicious, especially the *toucinho do céu*, which literally means "the lard of heaven."

Pousada de Santa Maria (P)
7330 Marvão
Tel: (045) 9 32 01
This picturesque *pousada* nestled in a whitewashed village with steep, narrow streets offers a total change of scene. Guests should not miss dinner in the dining room to catch the fabulous sunset.

Estalagém de Monsaraz (H)
Largo de São Bartolomeu, 5, 7200 Monsaraz
Tel: (066) 5 51 12.
This hotel's architecture matches the surrounding whitewashed, fortified town. The interior is very tastefully decorated yet natural. Rooms with country-style furniture look out over the valley. The fireplaces and exposed beams in the lounges are reminders that winters in Alentejo are harsh.

Castelo de Milfontes (TH)
Margarida de Castro de Almeida
Vila Nova de Milfontes, 7555 Odemira
Tel: (083) 9 61 08
Guests reach this enchanted waterside *castelo* by crossing a drawbridge. The rooms in the family residence boast fine old furniture and the food here is terrific. The simple yet elegant welcome is unforgettable.

Casa dos Arcos (TH)
Maria Jardím Hintze Ribeiro
Praça Martím Afonso de Sousa, 16, 710 Vila Viçosa
Tel: (068) 9 85 18
(see p. 209)
This beautiful house decorated with frescoes is near the royal palace. Spacious rooms and a Renaissance loggia.

Casa de Peixinhos (TH)
José Dionísio Melo e Faro Passanha
7160 Vila Viçosa
Tel: (068) 9 84 72
(see p. 208)
Cosy rooms await in this whitewashed seventeenth-century manor with bright ochre trimming. The arcaded patio is fragrant with the scent of orange trees.

RESTAURANTS

Áquias d'Ouro
Rossio Marquês de Pombal, 7100 Estremoz
Tel: (068) 33 33 26
Considered the best restaurant in town, the specialties here include succulent lamb dishes. Not to be missed is the *borrego com mioleiras guisado*, a lamb stew with brains.

Adega do Isaías
Rua do Almeida 23, 7100 Estremoz
Tel: (068) 2 23 18
This bistro specializes in every form of pork imaginable, from ears—*orelhas*—to baked feet—*chispes assados no forno*—and feet prepared with coriander—*pézhinos do porco de coentrada.*

Cozhina de São Humberto
Rua da Moeda 39, 7000 Évora
Tel: (066) 2 42 51
Delicious regional cooking with terrific local wines served in beautiful, whitewashed, vaulted dining rooms. The red Reguengos goes perfectly with the *arroz de pato cozido*, rice with duck and chorizo.

Fialho
Travessa das Mascarenhas 16, 7000 Évora
Tel: (066) 2 30 79
This well-known restaurant specializes in *borrego assado*, roast lamb, and herb salads the way only Alentejanos know how to make them.

Jardím do Paço
Rua Augusto Filipe Simões, 2, 7000 Évora
Tel: (066) 74 43 00
The Cadavals have opened their palace's gardens near the Dos Lóios monastery to the public. The small restaurant is a delightful spot to have lunch or a refreshing drink.

HUNTING

Herdade da Pereira
João Fiuza da Silveira
Apartado 99, 7000 Évora
Tel: (066) 2 44 61
João Fiuza da Silveira organizes hare-hunting expeditions with greyhounds on his huge estate. The riders meet afterwards to share an excellent meal in the stud farm's hunting room.

Vale do Manantio
To make reservations:
Sodarca, rua de São Paulo, 12-2°, 1200 Lisboa
Tel: (01) 347 10 11
The landowners here organize hunting expeditions on their extensive Vale do Manantio estate near Moura in the Beja region. The land on the banks of the Guadiana is teeming with game such as partridge, pheasant, and hare. Hunters are lodged in a comfortable house on the estate.

ARTS AND CRAFTS

Casa de Artes e Ofícios
Rua de Évora, 160, Igrejinha, 7040 Arraiolos
Tel: (066) 4 71 31
The rugs in this workshop are patterned after beautiful old models. The choice is wide and shoppers can buy directly from the workshop.

Tapetes de Arraiolos Kalifa
Rua Alexandre Herculano 44/46, 7040 Arraiolos
Tel: (066) 4 14 27
This carpet workshop is very careful about respecting traditional designs and wools.

Joaquím Correia Pereira
7035 Azaruja
Tel: (066) 9 71 92
Cork creations are sold directly from this craftsman's workshop. Many of his perfectly made pieces have been acquired by the Estremoz municipal museum.

Irmãos Flores
Rua das Meiras 8,
7100 Estremoz
Tel: (068) 2 42 39
Maria Inácia Flores and her sister, Perpétua, shape, bake, and paint beautiful figurines and large statues of the Virgin Mary along with other saints dear to the Portuguese.

Irmãos Ginja
Municipal Museum
Largo D. Dinis, 7100 Estremoz
Tel: (068) 2 27 83
The workshop of Afonso and Arlindo Ginja is located on the premises of the municipal museum. They make copies of old works in the collections as well as create their own pieces in the same personal spirit.

Portalegre Tapestry Factory
Fabrica Real, Parque da Corredura, 7300 Portalegre
Tel: (045) 2 32 83
Paintings are reproduced here on tightly woven tapestries. Jean Lurçat, Vieira da Silva, Manuel Cargaleiro, and many other artists have chosen this famous workshop to execute their cartoons. It is open to and accepts orders from the public.

Loja Misette
Rua do Celeiro Monsaraz,
7200 Reguengos de Monsaraz
Tel: (066) 5 21 79
(see p. 214)
Misette Nielsen has *mantas*, brightly colored traditional woolen blankets, and *trapos*, very popular, colorful, Alentejo-style rugs made of cotton offcuts, woven in her workshop. They are available at her boutiques in Monsaraz and Estremoz.

Oleiros São José
Estrada de Monsaraz,
7200 São Pedro do Corval (near Reguengos de Monsaraz)
Tel: (066) 3 14 63
Traditional terra-cotta ceramics are made in this workshop, which has been in the Fialho family for nearly four hundred years.

FAIRS AND MARKETS

Castro Verde
This fair, which is held the second Sunday of October, is an event. Traditional items that are gradually vanishing from everyday life can be found here, such as saddlery, painted carts, and wooden spoons. Lots of nostalgia.

Estremoz
(see p. 192)
The Saturday morning market on the Rossio is very picturesque. Items available here include all kinds of ceramics, loose-fitting greatcoats with fox fur collars, cork boxes, tablecloths made of Nisa embroidered felt and, of course, those wonderful painted terra-cotta figurines.

Évora
The big annual fair is held during the second half of June. All of Alentejo's craftsmen come here to offer their wares, including cork items, painted wooden furniture, and rustic ceramics.

MUSEUM

Municipal Museum
Largo de D. Dinis
7100 Estremoz
Tel. (town hall): (068) 2 27 33
This small museum of folk art and traditions displays beautiful *bonecos* (figurines) the famous *púcaros* (pitchers) and marble sculptures from Estremoz.

THE ALGARVE

WHERE TO STAY

Vila Joya (H)
Praia da Galé, 8200 Albufeira
Tel: (089) 59 17 95
Maria José Salavisa decorated the lounges and lavish bedrooms in this Moorish-style hotel that is surrounded by a garden and overlooks the sea. The terrace is a wonderful spot for a sunset dinner. *Caldeirada* (fish stew) and shellfish are rightly popular dishes.

Estalagém da Cegonha (H)
8100 Vilamoura (near Albufeira)
Tel: (089) 30 25 77
The riding ring of this congenial old farm makes it a popular spot with horseback riders, who also appreciate the nearby Vilamoura equestrian center.

Casa de Lumena (H)
Praca Alexandre Herculano, 27,
8000 Faro
Tel: (089) 80 19 90
This dignified residence is in the heart of Faro. The furniture here has been chosen with care. Meals are delightful in the shade of the patio's vine arbor.

Quinta de Benatrite (TH)
John Philip Oliver
Santa Barbara de Nexe, 8000 Faro
Tel: (089) 9 04 50
Shaded by large trees, this warm, friendly country house is tastefully decorated.

Casa de São Gonçalo (H)
Rua Cãndido dos Reis,
73, 8600 Lagos
Tel: (082) 76 21 71
This old, carefully furnished dwelling is a charming place to stay in the historic town of Lagos. The flower-bedecked patio's centerpiece is a fountain. Having breakfast in this oasis is a real pleasure.

Estalagém Abrigo
da Montanha (H)
8550 Monchique
A great base for exploring the gorgeous back country, the rooms and flowery terrace of this cosy mountain inn have unforgettable views. Local products are used to make regional dishes such as *assadura*, succulent grilled pork.

Hotel Bela Vista (H)
Avenida Tomás Cabreira, Praia da Rocha, 8500 Portimão
Tel: (082) 2 40 55
This delightful Oriental-look resort boasts a minaret and palm trees that seem planted on the beach. The tasteful interior is decorated with beautiful azulejo panels.

Fortaleza do Beliche (H)
8650 Sagres
Tel: (082) 6 41 24
A little jewel overlooking the sea is a recollection of the Age of Discoveries. The fortress houses a few rooms, a small chapel and a good restaurant specializing in grilled fish dishes.

Pousada do Infante (P)
8650 Sagres
Tel: (082) 6 42 22
The words of the poet Camões, "Where land ends and the sea begins," could describe this wonderful *pousada*. Each room overlooks the ocean and the steep cliffs.

Pousada de São Brás (P)
8150 São Brás de Alportel
Tel: (089) 84 23 05
This *pousada* is surrounded by a garden brimming with flowers and has a great view. The kitchen serves good local dishes such as *berbigões abertos à algarvia*, fresh casseroled shellfish, and *torta de amendoa*, a rolled almond pastry.

Quinta do Caracol (TH)
João Marcelo Viegas
São Pedro, 8800 Tavira
Tel: (081) 2 24 75
A few little houses with character are very well laid-out in a flower-filled garden. The view stretches to the sea and mountains.

RESTAURANTS

Cidade Velha
Rua Domingos Guieiro, 19,
8000 Faro
Tel: (89) 2 71 45
This restaurant near the cathedral is one of the best in Faro. The house specialty *lulas recheadas*, squid stuffed with lard is served in the beautiful dining rooms with vaulted brick ceilings.

Alpendre
Rua António Barbosa Viana 71,
8600 Lagos
Tel: (082) 76 27 0
Outstanding cuisine makes this luxurious restaurant one of the best-known addresses in the Algarve. A wide range of excellent fish and seafood dishes are available.

O Avenida
Avenida José da Costa,
8100 Loulé
Tel: (089) 6 21 06
This country-style inn located in the center of Loulé has an outstanding reputation.
They serve an Algarve specialty called *ameijoas na cataplana*, clams cooked slowly with raw ham.

A Lanterna
Estrada 125, intersection of Ferragudo and Parchal
8500 Portimão
Tel: (082) 2 39 48
This country-style restaurant is considered to have some of the best food in the Algarve. The recommended dish is *caldo rico de peixe*, a mouth-watering fish soup.

Alfredo's
Rua Pé da Cruz, 10,
8500 Portimão
Tel: (082) 2 29 54
The leading restaurant in Portimão is popular with regulars who come here to enjoy good Portuguese cooking. The *sopa de peixes*, fish soup, and *pescada marinheiro*, are especially tasty.

MUSEUM

Estói Palace
Estói, 8000 Faro
Tel: (089) 8 72 82
For guided tours:
Faro City Hall.
Tel: (089) 82 20 42
This magnificent palace looms up in the middle of stepped Portuguese baroque gardens laid out in the late nineteenth century. The palace and grounds are being restored and will be opened to the public.

The list of *feiras*—fairs—and *romarias*—religious festivals held in honor of a patron saint—is long, especially for the north. They are celebrated with processions, dances, parades and, of course, fireworks, which were brought back from China during the Age of Discoveries. The following is a selection of some of these festivals.

FEBRUARY OR MARCH, before Ash Wednesday
Parades with floats and floral display competitions in **Ovar, Torres Vedras,** and **Loulé.**

MARCH OR APRIL during Holy Week
Braga: the stations of the cross are re-enacted in churches and throughout the city. The very solemn processions of penitents are similar to the ones in Seville.

MAY
Barcelos, 3: one of the biggest festivals in the north. Procession of the festival of crosses, folk dancing, and a crafts exhibition with a wide choice of ceramics.
Fátima, 12 and 13: Portugal's biggest pilgrimage takes place on the 12th and 13th of every month from May to October. The devout walk here from all over the country, as is done for the festival of Santiago de Compostela.

JUNE
Amarante: the first weekend. Major festival of Sao Gonçalo, the saint who encourages weddings.
Lisbon: popular saints' days: Saint Anthony's Day is celebrated on the 24th and Saint John's on the 25th. There are musical parades throughout the city. The old neighborhoods are decorated with garlands and people dance in improvised outdoor cafés.
Braga, 21 to 24: Saint John's Festival. Costume parade, procession of folk groups, fireworks.
Vila do Conde, 16 to 24: The *mordomas*, women from Minho wearing the famous gold jewelry and lace of their regional costumes, parade in honor of Saint John.
Porto, 23 and 24: Saint John's Festival. Dancing and singing around a bonfire while eating grilled meats and sardines washed down with *vinho verde.*
Évora, 23 to 29: festival of Saint John. Crafts and music.
São Pedro de Sintra, 29: Saint Peter's Day. A huge fair with antiques, crafts, and second-hand goods.

JULY
Campo Maior, early July: in theory the *festas de povos*, festivals of the people, are held every seven years. The next one is scheduled for 1995. The entire city is decked out with fascinating paper cut-out decorations of birds, flowers, animals, and garlands. Every street becomes enchanted.
Vila Franca de Xira, the first weekend. The big festival of the Ribatejo is called the *colete encarnado* the red vest. The *campinos*—herdsmen—march through the streets. Other merry-making includes running of the bulls, bullfights, folk dances, and feasts of grilled sardines.
Guimarães, early July: festivals of São Torcato. Processions and an international folk festival.
Tomar, first half of July in odd years: festival of the Tabuleiros, one of the most famous celebrations in the country. The young women wear headpieces equal to their own height called *tabuleiro*s, made of stacked loaves of bread decorated with flowers. Dancing, bullfights, and fireworks are part of the festivities.

AUGUST
Viana do Castelo, third week: *romaria* of Our Lady of the Agony.
The most famous festival in Minho features the area's most beautiful costumes, a procession, a bullfight, a parade of giants and dwarfs, fireworks, and a folk dance festival.

SEPTEMBER
Palmela, first Sunday: wine harvest festival. Blessing of the grapes, folklore, music, fireworks.
Lamego, beginning of the month: *romaria* da Senhora dos Remédios. Processions with statues showing episodes from the Virgin Mary's life. Floral display competitions.

OCTOBER
Castro Verde, second half of the month: all kinds of items used by traditional farming society can be bought at this very lively fair.

NOVEMBER
Golega, first half of the month: Saint Martin's Day. The national Lusitanian horse fair. Parade, teamwork and jumping competitions, dressage, and auctions.

BIBLIOGRAPHY

The bibliography of books in English on Portugal is extensive and the selection given here is by no means exhaustive. While we have listed mainly English works or translations, we are also including some important titles (especially works cited in this book) that will be useful to readers with a sufficient understanding of French or Portuguese.

GUIDES

Published annually unless otherwise noted.

Baedeker's Portugal. 2nd Ed. London: The Automobile Association.
Blue Guide Portugal. New York: W. W. Norton.
Cadogan Guide Portugal. London: Cadogan Books.
Fodor's Portugal, Including Madeira and the Azores. New York: Fodor's Travel.
Frommers, Portugal. New York: Prentice Hall.
Guia de Portugal. Lisbon: Biblioteca Nacional de Lisboa, 1927. Modern edition, Fundação Calouste Gulbenkian, 1988.
Guide des hôtels de charme d'Espagne et du Portugal. Paris: Rivages.
Karen Brown's Portuguese Country Inns & Pousadas. London: Harrap Columbus.
Portugal's Pousada Route, Stuart Moss. Lisbon: Vista Ibérica publicacões, 1992.
Real Guide: Portugal. New York: Prentice Hall, 1989.
Rough Guide Portugal. London: The Rough Guides.
Turismo no espaço rural, Direcção Geral do Turism, Lisboa. A guide to *turismo de habitação* in English, French, and German.

TRAVEL AND MISCELLANEOUS LITERATURE

BECKFORD, William, *Recollections of an Excursion to the Monasteries of Alcobaça and Batalha.* Centaur Press, 1972.
CHANTAL, Suzanne, *La Caravelle et les Corbeaux.* Paris: Plon, 1948. *Portugal.* Paris: Sun, 1987.
DÉON, Michel, Jacques CHARDONNE and **Paul MORAND,** *Le Portugal que j'aime*. Paris: Sun, 1960.
GIRAUDOUX, Jean, *Portugal*. Paris: Grasset, 1958.
KAPLAN, Marion, *The Portuguese: the Land and its People*. London: Penguin, 1991.
KYRIA, Pierre, *Lisbonne*. Paris: Champ Vallon, 1985. *La Mort blanche*. Paris: Fayard, 1972.
LÉGLISE-COSTA, Philippe and **Pierre,** *Le Portugal*, Romain Pages, 1990.
LOPES, Fernão, *The English in Portugal.* London: Aris and Phillips, 1988.
MACAULAY, Rose, *They Went to Portugal*. London: Penguin, 1985.
MORAND, Paul, *Le Prisonnier de Sintra.* Paris: Livre de Poche, 1974. *Lorenzaccio ou le retour du proscrit.* Paris: Livre de Poche, 1977. *Bains de mer.* Paris: Arléa, 1991.
PINA-CABRAL, João, *Sons of Adam, Daughters of Eve.* Clarendon Press, 1986.
TABUCCHI, António, *Requiem*. Paris: Bourgois, 1993.
T'SERSTEVENS, A., *L'Itinéraire portugais*. Paris: Grasset, 1940.
VOLTAIRE, *Candide or Optimism.* Trans. by John Butt. London: Penguin, 1983.

HISTORY

BIRMINGHAM, David, *A Concise History of Portugal,* Cambridge University Press, 1992.
BOXER, C. R., *The Portuguese Seaborne Empire 1415–1825.* London: Hutchinson, 1977.
CHANTAL, Suzanne, *La Vie quotidienne au Portugal après le tremblement de terre.* Paris: Hachette, 1962.

LIVERMORE, Harold, *A New History of Portugal,* Cambridge University Press, 1969.
NOWELL, Charles, *A History of Portugal.* Van Nostrand, 1952.
OLIVEIRA, A. H., Marques de *History of Portugal,* 2 vol. Columbia, 1972.
PAYNE, S. G., *History of Spain and Portugal.* University of Wisconsin Press, 1973.
READ, Jan, *The Moors in Spain and Portugal,* London: Faber and Faber, 1974.
URE, John, *Henry the Navigator.* London: Constable and Co., 1977.

ART AND ILLUSTRATED BOOKS

BINNEY, Marcus, *Country Manors of Portugal,* London: Scala Books, 1987.
BLUNT, Anthony, Ed., *Baroque and Rococo Architecture and Decoration.* London: Paul Elek, 1978.
CARITA, Helder and **Homem CARDOSO,** *Portuguese Gardens.* London: Antique Collector's Club.
GIL, Júlio and **Augusto CABRITA,** *The Finest Castles in Portugal.* Scala Books, 1986.
GRUBER, Alain, Ed., *The History of Decorative Arts: The Renaissance and Mannerism in Europe.* New York, Abbeville Press, 1995.
QUIGNARD, Pascal, *La Frontière*. Chandeigne, 2nd Edition 1992. Inspired by the Fronteira Palace. A deluxe edition.
DE STOOP, Anne, *Demeures portugaises dans les environs de Lisbonne*. Weber Civilização, 1986. *Palais et manoirs, le Minho*. To be published by Éditions du Seuil (Paris) in 1995.
TEROL, Marylène, *Azulejos à Lisbonne*. Paris: Hervas, 1992.
WHOL, Helmut and **Alice,** *Portugal.* Scala Books, 1983.
WATSON, Walter CRUM, *Portuguese Architecture.* London: Archibald Constable, 1908.

PORTUGUESE LITERATURE

Classics:

CAMÕES, Luís De, *The Lusiads*. Penguin, 1985.
QUEIROZ, José Maria Eça De, *The Maias*, Dent, 1986.
PESSOA, Fernando, Selected Poems.London: Penguin, 1988. *The Book of Disquiet.* London: Serpent's Tail, 1982.

Other major classic writers that should be mentioned include: **Camilo Castelo Branco**, **Fernão Mendes Pinto**, and **Aquilino Ribeiro**.

Contemporary:

PIRES, José Cardoso, *Ballad of Dogs' Beach.* Dent, 1986.
SARAMAGO, José, *Baltasar and Blimunda.* London: Cape, 1988; *The Year of the Death of Ricardo Reis.* Harcourt Brace, 1994; *The Stone Raft.* Harcourt Brace, 1986.
TORGA, Miguel, *Tales From The Mountain,* Fort Bragg, California: Q.E.D. Press, 1991.

Other important contemporary Portuguese writers include: **Alexandre Almeida Faria**, **Agustina Bessa Luís, Maria Judite De Carvalho**, **Vergílio Ferreira**, **Nuno Júdice**, **António Lobo Antunes**, **Eduardo Lourenço, Sophia De Mello Breyner**, **Fernando Namora**, **Vitorino Nemésio**, **Luis Miguel Queirós**, and **Jorge De Sena**.

COOKBOOKS, WINE, AND ENTERTAINING

BRADFORD, Sarah, *The Story of Port.* London: Christie's Wine Publications, 1983.
LIDDELL, Alex and **Janet PRICE,** *Port Wine Quintas of the Douro.* Preface by Serena Sutcliffe. London: Philip Wilson, 1992.
MODESTO, Maria De Lourdes, *Cozinha traditional portuguesa.* Verbo, 1982.
READ, Jan, *The Wines of Portugal.* London: Faber and Faber, 1987.
MAYSON, Richard, *Portugal's Wines and Wine Makers.* Ebury Press, 1992.
SILVA, Jorge Tavares Da, *La Cuisine portugaise de tradition populaire.* Le Guide des Connaisseurs, 1991.
VIEIRA, Edite, *The Taste of Portugal.* London: Robinson.

Figures in italics refer to the Visitor's Guide.

ACKNOWLEDGMENTS

I would like to thank everyone in Portugal who has welcomed me with such warmth and hospitality for so many years, especially John de Stoop, Martine Teixeira Guerra and the architect António Teixeira Guerra, as well as all the friends or friends of friends who have always opened their doors and offered their friendship to me. All my gratitude goes to Isabel Palha, Helena Vaz da Silva and Miguel Veiga for their invaluable help and to Claire Baudoin for all the people she managed to contact.

I would like to thank Nathalie Bailleux, Florence Picard and José da Costa for their help on this work in France. Let me also thank Ly Mei Tran, Isabelle de Béru and Virginie Leroux for their active enthusiasm.

Michel Chandeigne, director of the Librairie Portugaise, helped me with his advice and gave suggestions for writing the bibliography. Maria Teresa Salgado of the library at the Centre Culturel Calouste Gulbenkian assisted with the research.

The Portuguese Trade and Tourism Office, its former director Mr. Armando Calvão Rocha and his assistant Ms. Maria Héléna Moura were a constant source of support.

Lastly I would like to thank the City Tour car rental agency in Lisbon for making it easier to travel in Portugal.

Jérôme Darblay and Caroline Champenois would like to thank everyone who so warmly welcomed them to Portugal. They are especially thinking of Miguel Amaral Neto, Claire Baudoin, Countess Carmito Capodilista, Isabel de Carvalho, José Castro Pereira, Vera Espírito Santo et Manrico Iachia, Pierre Léglise-Costa, Carlos Tavares Gravato, Luis Uscha and Léonie Moschner for her helpful assistance. They are also thinking of everyone who gave priceless advice and opened the doors of their homes: Marina and Luís Aguiam, Maria Augusta and António Julio d'Alpuim, Manuel and Madalena Almeida de Abecassis, Maria de Sommer d'Andrade, Maria Emília Barros Lamas, Júlio Bastos, Françoise Baudry, Till and Catarina Becker de Freitas, Marie-Odile Briet and Hervé Tullet, Philippe Bustorff, Count Calheiros, Manuel and Maria Zinha Campilho, Maria do Carmo Uva, Count Guy de Casteja and his daughter Gaelle, Manuel de Castro Tavares Veiga, Sylvie Flaure and Sylvie Grumbach, António and Bénédicte Fragoso, João Fiuza da Silveira, Jean Loup le Forestier, Max and Eleonor Forte, the ambassador of France and Mme. Grenier, Pedro Guimarães, Fernando Guedes, Lídia Jorge, José Lobo, Manuel Bernardo Lobo, dom Lourenço de Almeida, Gustavo Ludgero de Castro, Pedro Luz, Countess Mafalda d'Anadia, Jean-Pierre Mahot de la Quérantonnais and Colombe Pringle, Mark and Arturo, João Marquès Pinto, Marta de Mello Breyner, Leila Mendes, Mizette, Ms. Moura of the Portugal Office of Trade and Tourism, Felipa Morais and Héléna Amaral, Florence Picard, ambassador Antonio Pinto de Mesquita, Julio Pomar, Mr. and Mrs. Eric S.G. Reid, Alistair and Gillyane Robertson, Baron von Rosen and his sister Christina, Ana Salazar, Martin Saldanha, the little orphans of Santo Antão do Tojal, Ms. Scheider, Manuel Carlos Seara Carvalhinha Alves Costa, Álvaro Siza Vieira, Dom Fernando de Souza Albuquerque, the Marquis and Marquise de Sousa Holstein, Helena Corrêa de Sá, José and Julia Teixeira de Queiroz, Helena Vaz da Silva, Countess Vill'Alva.

The publishers would like to thank Mário Soares, president of Portugal, who agreed to write the foreword of this book. They would also like to thank the owners of all the homes, institutions and boutiques mentioned in this book as well as Christian Auscher, Nathalie Bailleux, Maria de Lourdes Belchior and Nicole de Barbuat, Mme. Barelier, Claire Baudoin, José Manuel dos Santos, the ambassador of France and Mme Grenier, Pierre Léglise-Costa, Anne Lima, the ambassador of Portugal in France José Maria Maçedo, Teresa Mendes, Maria Helena Moura, Elza Neto, Bernard Nicolas, Florence Picard, Henrique de Queiroz Nazareth, Alistair Robertson, Armando Calvão Rocha, Filipe Rocha da Silva, Eduardo Rogado-Dias, Hermano Sanchez Ruivo, Maria José Salavisa, Maria Teresa Salgado, the consul of Portugal in France José Tadeu Soares, Helena Vaz da Silva, Monique Veaute and Miguel Veiga.